Can a Catholic Be a Democrat?

Also from Sophia Institute Press®
by David R. Carlin:

The Decline and Fall of the Catholic Church in America

David R. Carlin

Can a Catholic Be a Democrat?

How the Party I Loved Became the Enemy of My Religion

SOPHIA INSTITUTE PRESS®
Manchester, New Hampshire

Cover design by Theodore Schluenderfritz

Sophia Institute Press®
Box 5284, Manchester, NH 03108
1-800-888-9344
www.sophiainstitute.com

Library of Congress Cataloging-in-Publication Data

Carlin, David (David R.)
Can a Catholic be a Democrat? : how the Party I loved became the enemy of my religion / David R. Carlin.
p. cm.
Includes bibliographical references.
ISBN-13: 978-1-933184-19-7 (pbk. : alk. paper)
1. Christianity and politics — Catholic Church. 2. Christianity and politics — United States. 3. Democratic Party (U.S.) I. Title.

BX1793.C32 2006
324.2736 — dc22 2006019075

06 07 08 09 10 9 8 7 6 5 4 3 2 1

This book is dedicated to:

David R. Carlin, Sr. (1909-1980)
Marion McGetrick Carlin (1911-1989)
Maureen Carlin Fitzgerald (1945-2003)

Contents

Part II
The Party and the Church Are Irreconcilable

Appendices

Publisher's Note

A few months ago, I mentioned to a conservative Catholic friend that we planned to entitle this book *Can a Catholic Be a Democrat?*

My friend shot back, "Can a Catholic be a Republican?"

That's a fair question, but it's the subject of a different book. For our purpose here is not to endorse particular candidates, affect elections, or even support a particular party. (Like most Catholics today, we don't agree completely with any of them — and we don't even agree with all of our author's political assumptions.)

Our effort transcends prudential judgments about war and peace, wealth and taxes, and the persons vying for office today; it's deeper than any particular issue, contest, or political philosophy.

In a word, in publishing this book our purpose is Catholic. We hope by means of it to help Catholics see clearly the political choices they face, so that they can prudently work for policies consistent with the fundamental truths of the Catholic Faith.

As this book goes to press, we hear reports of shifts in the electorate. Stalwart conservatives and even many Republican moderates have begun to question their allegiance to the GOP; lifelong Democrats find it ever harder to vote Democratic. Catholics in both parties have wandering eyes and are open to being courted by political parties they might never have supported before.

To help them choose, and to help the parties themselves understand Catholics better and win their votes, author David Carlin here shows what it means to be Catholic in the public square. He explains the fundamental policies that Catholics must support and identifies ones that Catholics will never abide.

His arguments might not lead you to a more Catholic party, but they will help you make your party less hostile to the beliefs of Catholics.

And — whether you're Catholic or not — if you seek to win elections, you need to do just that. For in many elections, Catholics are the swing voters who determine the outcome.

The party that hears Carlin's voice today will win elections tomorrow.

Acknowledgments

In writing this book I have been aided by many people. First of all, thanks to Todd Aglialoro, my remarkably talented editor at Sophia Institute Press, who worked on both this book and my previous book *(The Decline and Fall of the Catholic Church in America)*. Thanks to Professor John Quinn of Salve Regina University, who read an earlier draft of this book and supplied many helpful comments. Thanks to former Rhode Island state Representative Spencer Dickinson, who also read an earlier draft and was the first to suggest an autobiographical framework. Thanks to the late Bill Kinnaman, a teaching colleague of mine who was both a professor of philosophy and an Evangelical minister. A month or two before his death Bill made a number of helpful comments on my "Liberal Christianity" appendix. And thanks above all to the woman who was my earliest political partner and has been the great love of my life: my wife, Maureen.

Preface

"We love our friends, but we love the truth more."
Aristotle, *Nicomachean Ethics*

This book is a complaint from a disappointed lover. It's possible to love institutions as well as persons, and I once loved the Democratic Party — the party of Franklin Roosevelt and his New Deal liberals, the party that once upon a time did wonderful things for blue-collar Americans like my parents, the party that helped immigrant Catholics and their children (my parents again) become real Americans. Later on I'll tell the story of my love affair with the party and my gradual disillusionment, but for now let me simply record the fact that I'm writing with the political equivalent of a broken heart.

I haven't taken up with another party; that is to say, I haven't become a Republican. In fact, I haven't yet left the Democratic house: I'm still a registered Democratic voter, I always vote in Democratic primaries here in Rhode Island, and I continue to participate actively in Democratic politics at the local level. But at the national level, and to a limited extent even at the state level, I find less and less to love in my party as it is today, and sometimes I have no choice but to vote for Republican candidates for high office. I think, or at least I hope, that someday the Democratic Party will once again become a loveable thing. But it takes a long, long time for a political party to change its orientation, and since I'm now in my late sixties, I doubt that the change I look for will take place in my lifetime. I expect to die a Democrat, albeit a very unhappy one.

The reasons for my unhappiness — and not just mine but the unhappiness of millions — I will explain in detail in the following pages. But a short way of putting the thing is to say that in the great "Culture War" currently going on between old-fashioned Christians and anti-Christian secularists, over issues such as abortion, same-sex marriage, euthanasia, and the role of religion in society, my Democratic Party has opted to side with the secularists.

I write this book as a Catholic who fears for the future of Christianity in America, but also as a Democrat who fears for the future of the Democratic Party. Already it has experienced a great decline, a decline that first became clear in the election of 1980, when Ronald Reagan, with great help from religious conservatives (many of them Democrats), won the White House and the Republicans gained control of the U.S. Senate.

True, since that time the Democrats have experienced episodes of prosperity, Bill Clinton's presidency being the most notable, but the long-term trend is clear. The Democrats used to be America's number-one party; they're now the number-two party; and if they continue to alienate religious and moral-conservative voters, they're likely to remain number two for a long time to come.

As the Civil War approached, the Democrats took the wrong position on slavery, and they found themselves, except for a few brief episodes of prosperity, America's minority party from the election of Abraham Lincoln in 1860 until the election of Franklin Roosevelt in 1932. At the time of the Great Depression of the 1930s, the Republicans took the wrong position on the social and economic welfare responsibilities of the federal government, and they remained America's number-two party until the coming of Reagan and Newt Gingrich in the 1980s and '90s. Today the Democrats are taking the wrong position on morality and religion, which may doom them to remain America's minority party until well into the twenty-first century.

I remember reading a magazine article in the early 1960s, a report of an interview with William Faulkner. The Civil Rights struggle was growing very intense at the time, and the interviewer posed to the famous novelist a hypothetical question: If it came to a shooting war between blacks and whites, which side would Faulkner take? As anybody knows who has read his novels, Faulkner had great sympathy for blacks and the injustices they suffered. Nonetheless he said that in such a war he would fight on the side of the whites. Why? Because, he said, although whites might have committed great crimes against blacks, in the last analysis the whites were *his people*.

I recognize that traditional Christians, whether Catholic or Protestant, have historically often done dreadful things — been guilty of violence, injustice, prejudice. But whatever their history of crimes and ignorance (and even in our day they're not all saints), old-fashioned Christians are "my people." I'm one of them, so it's quite natural that I should be on their side in the Culture

War. Besides, the secularists don't have a sterling track record themselves,[1] and even if I had no formal attachment to Christianity, I suspect I would feel bound to support the Christian side in the Culture War because, bad as Christians have often been, a world dominated by secularists would be even worse.

In this book I offer no new information. I'm working with a set of facts everybody already knows — at least everybody who has been paying a moderate degree of attention to American politics and religion in recent decades. My role is that of the detective in a mystery story: I know the same clues known by everybody else working on the case, but I happen to see a pattern the others missed.

I feel as if I should offer an apology (in both senses of that word) for the apparent excess of appendices — five of them — in this volume. On the one hand, the topics covered therein didn't seem quite *essential* to the argument presented in the book. On the other hand, they were necessary for the *fullness* of that argument. Hence my compromise: drop them from the main text while keeping them in the book. I advise the reader to give almost as much attention to the appendices as to the main text.

And one last thing: I was, and remain, a bit embarrassed by the autobiographical content in this book. Autobiographies should be written by *important* people, and outside of the circle of my family and friends I'm rarely considered such. Nevertheless, if I'm not important as an individual, I might be important as an example of a *kind* of individual: the old hardcore Catholic Democrat who faces

[1] Consider the evil done by those twentieth-century anti-Christian faiths, Nazism and Communism.

a conflict between his party and his religion. The story I have to tell is a story that could be told by millions of others. We once loved the Democratic Party, but our love has waned as we have watched it drift farther and farther away from what it once was. We're critical of the party from the inside; we're not galvanized Republicans but authentic Democrats.

Introduction

How I Lost My Faith (in the Democratic Party)

I'm not certain when it first dawned on me that the Democratic Party had transformed itself into the pro-abortion party,[2] but I think it was early in the 1984 presidential campaign. Ronald Reagan was president, and he was a pro-life Republican (even though, when governor of California, he had signed a liberal abortion bill into law). A number of politicians — most notably, Jesse Jackson, Sen. Gary Hart, and former Vice President Walter Mondale — were fighting for the Democratic nomination, and all of them were openly pro-choice on abortion. For the first time it fully dawned on me how fundamentally committed to abortion my party had become.

At that time I was a Democratic member of the Rhode Island Senate, having first been elected in 1980. I was pro-life, as were most of my Democratic colleagues in the Rhode Island legislature; at the time there was nothing unusual about this. Of course, ever since *Roe v. Wade* in 1973, state legislatures had been taken out of

[2] In the course of this book I'll use the terms *pro-choice* and *pro-abortion* interchangeably.

the abortion-regulation business, so our convictions made little practical difference. But my conviction was nonetheless strong, and as I slowly awakened to the increasing pro-abortion character of my party, I began to feel conflicted.

I was a Catholic, and so I had the usual Catholic reasons for being opposed to abortion. I was also a philosopher — I had spent three years in the early sixties as a graduate student in philosophy at Notre Dame, and since that time I had been a college philosophy teacher — and so I had purely rational reasons, too, for thinking abortion to be morally wrong. On the other hand, I was an elected official belonging to America's pro-abortion party. Even if there seemed to be no political mechanism for ending abortion, how could I, simply as a matter of principle, continue my support for and affiliation with such a party?

I justified (or rationalized) my party identity with a number of arguments. The national Democratic Party might be pro-abortion, I said, but the Democratic Party isn't a monolithic thing controlled from some national center; rather, it's a federation made up of relatively autonomous state and local parties. My state and local parties were *not* pro-abortion parties, and almost all of my political activity was at the state and local levels. Moreover, if I were to leave the Democratic Party, where was I to go? The state Republican Party was no more pro-life than the state Democratic Party, and was arguably even less so. Or could I become an Independent? Given the bad luck that almost always attends an independent candidacy, that would surely mean losing my Senate position in the next election; and as a senator, while I could do nothing about abortion, I could make worthwhile contributions to other social-justice causes.

Besides, supporting the national Republican Party, it seemed to me, would be nothing but an empty gesture. For the only thing that would really advance the pro-life cause would be for the Supreme Court to overturn *Roe v. Wade;* yet I saw scant evidence that the national Republicans were truly determined to bring about this result. (My suspicion was later confirmed when a number of Reagan and Bush (senior) appointees to the Court — O'Connor, Kennedy, Souter — turned out to be supporters of *Roe.*)

And so, armed with these justifications, I remained a faithful if slightly chagrined Democratic partisan and politician. After all, it was more than a party to me: it was, and had been since my infancy, my home.

I was born in 1938 (the year of Munich, the year of the great New England hurricane), the oldest of three children in a working-class family in Pawtucket, Rhode Island — a gritty, blue-collar town, devoid of the loveliness that Plato says should surround children as they grow up. But there were those who loved it, and I was one of them. At the time of my birth, before the mills had all either folded or gone to the South, it was still one of New England's great textile towns; at one time it manufactured more thread than any other city in the world. Politically, the most important demographic group in the city was the Irish-Catholics: Democrats, of course; they controlled city hall — but not the mills or the banks.

My family was Irish-Catholic. Strictly speaking, my father was Scottish, but from a part of Scotland (Paisley, very near Glasgow) that abounded with Irish Catholics, refugees from poverty and the potato famine. After he had come to America as a child, he lived in an Irish-Catholic milieu, and so it was perfectly natural that he should marry my Irish-Catholic mother, the third youngest of eleven children. Until I was about ten years old, my father worked at the Pawtucket Boys' Club — one of my favorite hangouts — and after that he held jobs at the Providence Gas Company and, for many years, at the Narragansett Brewery. Although my mother was a high-school graduate, my father had dropped out of school after the eleventh grade, not uncommon in his day.

And my family was Democratic. They weren't directly involved in politics, but they voted for Democrats — especially for the greatest Democrat of them all, President Franklin Roosevelt — and they were friendly with a few of the local Democratic politicians. In addition to having a blue-collar ethnic Catholic profile that made him ripe to be a Democrat, my father directly benefitted from a number of FDR programs. As a young man, before his marriage, he spent time in Vermont as a member of the Civilian Conservation Corps. Years later, now a husband and father, he sometimes found himself temporarily out of work, and he was able to receive unemployment compensation (he was able to "collect," as the expression went). For many years in his working life, he benefitted from being a member of a labor union, a union that in all probability would not have existed had it not been for the Wagner Act (the National Labor Relations Act) of 1935. For my father, then, the New Deal wasn't simply an abstract ideal that he approved of. It was a concrete good.

I well remember a political lesson my father taught me when I was very young; I couldn't have been more than eight or nine. We're Democrats, he told me, because the Democrats are the party of the poor people, the Republicans are the party of the rich, and our family was poor.[3]

[3] In those days the word *poor* had a different meaning. Today to say that somebody is poor is to say that he belongs to an underclass plagued by unemployment, crime, drug addiction, bad manners, and worse. Back then it simply

My father's words to me that day provided the single most important lesson I've ever learned in politics. It cemented my attachment to the Democratic Party, and even though I realize that today's Democratic Party is no longer truly the party of the poor, it keeps me in the party today, more than a half-century later.

In 1989 I became the Senate Majority Leader, the highest position in the Senate and therefore one of the highest positions in Rhode Island state government. Three years later I decided to leave the state Senate and take a long-shot try at higher office: I became my party's candidate for the United States House of Representatives in my congressional district. I ran as a pro-life Democrat against a pro-choice Republican incumbent[4] who overwhelmingly outspent me, and my "strategy" was to hope that Democratic presidential candidate Bill Clinton would carry Rhode Island by a huge margin and drag me in on his coattails. Because of his pro-abortion commitments, I was less than a great fan of Clinton. In fact, that summer I wrote an op-ed piece that appeared in the *New York Times*, criticizing the Democratic National Convention (a Clinton-controlled event) for its refusal to allow Bob Casey, the pro-life governor of Pennsylvania, to give an address. And by this date the Republicans, with Bush's appointment of Clarence

meant that you weren't rich or nearly rich; it especially meant that you belonged to the class of blue-collar workers that made up the great majority of ethnic Catholics.

[4] This was Rep. Ronald Machtley, who, two years after defeating me, ran a losing campaign for governor of Rhode Island. He's now the president of Bryant University, in Smithfield, Rhode Island. The congressional seat I aspired to is now held by another Democrat, Rep. Patrick Kennedy (Teddy's son).

Thomas to the Supreme Court, had shown that they were getting truly serious about overturning *Roe v. Wade*. But I voted for Clinton on Election Day, since it seemed indecent to ride his coattails without even giving him a vote.

Clinton won Rhode Island, but not by the huge margin I had been counting on; even if he had, it probably wouldn't have mattered, for I was trounced by the incumbent. After that, I remained a registered Democrat and usually voted for Democrats at the local and state levels. But 1992 was the last time I voted for a Democrat for president.

Around this same time, my public life as a Catholic, such as it was, began to follow a similar line of progression. In the early eighties I got into the habit of writing political essays and submitting them to national magazines, especially two Catholic publications: *Commonweal* and the Jesuit journal *America*. In 1985 I began writing a regular monthly column for *Commonweal*, at first just on political subjects. Then as now, *Commonweal* had a reputation as a liberal Catholic magazine, and at that time I was a political liberal on just about every question except abortion, and I was a true-blue Democratic office-holder, so I fit the magazine's profile well.

But as the years went by, I started writing more about religious issues, and as I did so, I became more religiously conservative. I wrote a column in defense of the male-only priesthood, arguing that it's but one of many articles of Catholic faith that seem unreasonable in the eyes of the world, yet we nonetheless must believe. Of course, no good Catholic liberal — for whom the ordination of women was at or near the top of the reform agenda — would write such a column. I also ran afoul of *Commonweal*'s readership on those rare occasions when I wrote about the gay movement. For the most part, liberal Catholics in those days were not prepared to give homosexual conduct their stamp of approval; at the same time they had real sympathy for gays and lesbians, and they thought it was bad form, if not a downright lack of charity, to find fault with the movement and its agenda (which in those days did not yet include a vocal demand for same-sex marriage). But my career as a politician had left me suspicious of the gay movement, inasmuch as it pursued legislation designed not to protect basic civil rights but to use state power to endorse homosexuality.

I can't remember when exactly, but sometime rather late in my *Commonweal* career[5] I began writing about the abortion movement and the gay movement together, and for good measure I included the euthanasia movement. I called these three the "unholy trinity of contemporary secularism."[6] I no longer saw them as three separate issues; they were part of a single package, whose ultimate function was to marginalize traditional religion, especially old-fashioned Protestantism and Catholicism. If you were going to oppose one part of the unholy trinity, it seemed to me then, you had better oppose all three parts. It made no sense to say, as some

[5] My career at *Commonweal* would come to an end in 1997, when I received a letter from the editor informing me that my column was being discontinued. I never asked why, but my guess has always been that I had become too conservative, both socially and theologically; I was no longer sufficiently liberal for a magazine that wanted to maintain its venerable reputation for liberalism. I never complained about my dismissal, and I never resented it. It seems to me they were right to let me go. I wasn't a good fit anymore.

[6] For a definition of *secularism* as I use that term, see Appendix I.

pro-life Catholics did, "I'm against abortion, but I don't see anything wrong with the gay movement."

When I wrote about links between these movements, understand, I didn't mean to say that there was a vast anti-Christian conspiracy, a secularist politburo issuing weekly marching orders to the champions of abortion, same-sex marriage, and euthanasia. What I meant was that all three movements held values that are profoundly antithetical to traditional Christian values, and thus when they acted to promote their values, they were reinforcing one another's efforts whether they knew it or not — all to the ultimate detriment of Christianity.

Before long I came to see a link between the "unholy trinity of secularism" and the national Democratic Party, from which I was becoming estranged, and from there it took only a few more logical steps to arrive at the conclusions that I will argue for in the course of this book. For it had become plain to me that the Democratic Party, whose agenda now strongly supported abortion-on-demand, increasingly endorsed the goals of the gay movement, including same-sex marriage, and was showing signs of growing support for euthanasia, had come under the control of forces utterly opposed to all traditional Christianity and to Catholicism in particular. The happy marriage between my Church and my party had soured.

Where did it all go wrong? I think that the divorce was long in coming. Its roots can be traced back to the 1960s, to the social upheaval and the changes in American politics that transformed the Democratic Party of my youth into the thing it is today.

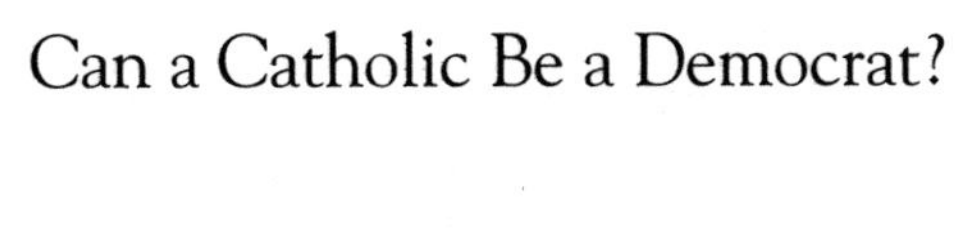

Can a Catholic Be a Democrat?

Part I

What the Democratic Party Has Become

Chapter 1

The Great Transformation, Part 1: Demise of the Political Machines

The Democratic Party of Franklin Roosevelt and the New Deal — strong, centralized, champion of the common man — was the ideal political party for typical Catholics of the 1930s and '40s. It was a patriotic party with a largely working-class base, and in those days the Catholic community in the United States, made up of immigrants and their children and grandchildren, was predominantly working-class and proudly patriotic.

But that wasn't all. The New Deal Democratic Party had a social and economic philosophy that largely coincided with the social teachings of the Church, as found in the papal encyclicals *Rerum Novarum* (1891) of Leo XIII and *Quadrigesimo Anno* (1931) of Pius XI. The New Deal followed a *via media* that avoided two extremes condemned in these documents: communism on the one hand, and laissez-faire capitalism on the other. The New Deal championed the rights of labor, including above all the right of workers to organize themselves in unions; at the same time, it had no intention of abolishing the rights of capital. Its view was that capital and labor should be something like equal partners, with neither having a clearly upper hand over the other. Its view also was that wealth and income ought to be far more evenly distributed in American society than they had been in recent times. These were views that might have been borrowed straight out of the social encyclicals of the popes.[7]

What's more, in the late 1940s, just after the death of Roosevelt, Harry Truman and other New Dealers transformed the Democratic Party, which during the war had been a great anti-fascist and anti-Nazi party, into a great anti-Communist party. The popes, of course, had always been intensely anti-Communist. What more could a Catholic want? I can think of no political party in modern times that in program and practice was more

[7] It's highly improbable that those who made up FDR's braintrust were great students of the social pronouncements of the popes. But an interesting case can be made that there was *some* borrowing. Beginning in the early years of the twentieth century, Monsignor John A. Ryan (1869-1945), inspired by Leo XIII's encyclical *Rerum Novarum*, developed in the course of many writings a distinctively Catholic approach to American social and economic questions, an approach that bore a strong resemblance to what was later to be the approach of the New Deal. In 1919 Ryan was the principal author of a social-economic reform program issued by the National Catholic Welfare Conference, a national organization of Catholic bishops that preceded the United States Catholic Conference. The official title of this program was "Program of Social Reconstruction," popularly known as "The Bishops' Program." In the 1936 presidential election campaign, Ryan made a radio address urging Catholics to vote for FDR; this was intended as a counter to the vehemently anti-FDR "radio priest," Fr. Charles Coughlin. See *Annotation: The Newsletter of the National Historical Publications and Records Commission* (March 2002).

congruent with the social teachings of the Catholic Church than the American Democratic Party of the 1930s and '40s. But it was not to last.

Crooked political machines begin to lose their grip

Until the years just after World War II, political "machines" and their "bosses" controlled many of America's cities. In the Democratic Party especially,[8] these machines were singularly powerful, the avenues through which virtually all political influence had to pass. They were also all more or less corrupt, maintaining power by means of graft and patronage and ticket-fixing.

As a child in Pawtucket, I once had a brief but vivid taste of our corrupt local machine, although at the time I certainly didn't understand what I was tasting. At the end of his workday at the Boys' Club in downtown Pawtucket, my father would sometimes stop for a drink at a popular men's bar just a few doors away from the Boys' Club. One day, when I was about nine or ten years old, I happened to be with him at the end of his workday, so — no doubt intending to contribute to my sociological education — he took me into the bar with him. We walked the entire length of the long, narrow barroom and went into a back room, where I saw something I had never seen before and wouldn't see again until I visited Nevada a couple of decades later — something whose existence I had never even suspected: many, many slot machines, with men standing in front of them, inserting coins and pulling levers. (Years later I learned that during World War II the Pawtucket

[8] There had been and still were some Republican machines, but by that late date most of the remaining machines were Democratic.

gambling industry had been very popular with sailors, who would often make the forty-mile trip from Newport to play the slots.)

The bar in question, a very well-known and usually very crowded establishment, was three or four hundred yards from City Hall and police-department headquarters (located, along with the fire department, on a street that the Democrats who controlled city government had recently renamed Roosevelt Avenue, in honor of their great hero in the White House). It is, of course, impossible that the police were unaware of the illegal slot machines or of the dozens of illegal bookies who operated in the city. Such illegal operations take place only if somebody at the mayor's office — and probably in the police department too — is getting paid off. In 1940s Pawtucket it might not have been a very handsome payment (not the kind, for instance, that drug dealers of later decades would pay to crooked cops), but it was enough to help keep the moving parts of the local political machine well lubricated. The same is true of the bribes and kickbacks that vendors who won city contracts undoubtedly paid to City Hall.

Nobody in my town doubted that the local Democratic machine, dominated by Irish-Catholics, was corrupt. From time to time, of course, the leaders of the machine would ritually deny any corruption, but nobody took these denials seriously. The good Catholic voters of Pawtucket didn't approve of this dishonesty, but at the same time it didn't overly disturb them. After all, what was the alternative to a crooked Democratic machine? A crooked Republican machine — and that had been tried already, during the decades prior to the Democratic ascendancy. When the choice is between two sets of crooks, doesn't it make sense to choose crooks who belong to your tribe? Besides, these voters were mostly immigrants and the children of immigrants, on the road to being fully Americanized. And one thing they knew about America was that petty — and sometimes not so petty — corruption had long been an essential ingredient in municipal politics, both Democratic and Republican.[9] This, apparently, was part of the American Way. So why fight it?

Nor is it likely that the corrupt Catholic politicians themselves had strong feelings of guilt. They were following the American Way. They went to church on Sundays. They were (mostly) faithful to their wives. They were responsible fathers. They gave a portion of their ill-gotten gains to charity. They helped poor people by means of their control of city hall. Moreover, how did their "wrongdoing" hurt anybody?[10]

If there were local machines, there were also statewide machines, which were little more than federations of local machines. Or to change the metaphor, if the bosses of the city machines were like feudal barons presiding over their urban baronies, the state boss was like a feudal king, a weak monarch whose strength (apart from his own personal barony) lay in his capacity to persuade all the barons to work together.

But after World War II, the golden age of these Democratic machines, which had just elected Franklin Roosevelt four times to the White House, was over. For one reason, the ethnic base of the machines was changing. Increasingly the base was moving out of the cities, where the machines had flourished, and into the

[9] For classic accounts of this, see Lincoln Steffens' *The Shame of the Cities* or his *Autobiography*, and the first two volumes of Theodore Dreiser's Frank Cowperwood trilogy. Also see sociologist Robert K. Merton's essay "Manifest and Latent Functions" in his *Social Theory and Social Structure* (Free Press, 1968).

[10] Of course, by undermining the principle of integrity in government, they hurt many people, just not in a direct, obvious, immediately tangible way.

suburbs. Increasingly too, the ethnic base was becoming middle-class and better educated; and unfortunately for machine politicians, Americans who are educated and middle-class have a rather low level of tolerance for local political corruption, even the relatively small-scale corruption practiced by churchgoing politicians.

And it wasn't just a matter of the machine's followers, but of its leaders also. In earlier decades, when other avenues of upward mobility were less than wide open to people whose families were recent arrivals in America, local politics attracted men of great natural talent: men who, if they had grown up in a society with greater equality of opportunity, would have become doctors, lawyers, engineers, professors, corporate executives, and so forth.

In the post–World War II era, however, things were changing radically. The new generation of immigrant stock Americans was more Americanized than their parents and grandparents, which meant that they were more prepared to leave the working class and enter the middle class. The GI Bill opened college education to those from lower socioeconomic groups who before the war would never have dreamed of going to college. Moreover, by sending veterans from blue-collar families to college, the GI Bill transformed the nation's idea of who should go to college. Now, regardless of class, anybody could go — that is, anybody who had the brains and determination to succeed — and those careers that depended on having a college education were likewise now open to all.

This left the leadership of local politics to men of inferior talent; thus, even if there was a theoretical possibility that the old machines could change their ways and adapt to the new postwar and increasingly suburban order of things, the high-quality leadership that could have engineered this adaptation was for the most part no longer available. The machines were doomed.

Demise of the Political Machines

The last hurrah of the machines came at the 1968 Democratic Convention, held in Chicago, where the now-feeble but surviving machine bosses were able to deliver a presidential nomination for one last time, to Hubert Humphrey. Lyndon Johnson's vice president at the time, Humphrey hadn't run in any of the presidential primaries (of which there were few in those days). Sen. Eugene McCarthy had run as an anti–Vietnam War candidate, and so had Sen. Robert Kennedy, jumping into the race in March just after McCarthy had almost defeated Lyndon Baines Johnson in the New Hampshire primary. Soon after New Hampshire and Kennedy's entry into the race, Johnson announced that he wouldn't be seeking another term. Both senators made strong showings in the primaries, but Kennedy was stronger, and, on the day he was assassinated, he had defeated McCarthy in the crucial California primary.

That the bosses would have delivered the nomination to Humphrey if Kennedy hadn't been shot is doubtful; Kennedy was popular not only with the Democratic masses but with many of the bosses as well. But McCarthy was a different story. His strength lay with middle- and upper-middle-class Democrats, with college and university students, with intellectuals and academics (including me, for I was a McCarthy supporter, and I worked strenuously on his rather insignificant Rhode Island campaign — insignificant because in those days the state didn't hold presidential primaries), with people who detested LBJ's war (I was one of those people too) — and in general with the kind of people who had little love for political bosses and were little loved by political bosses in turn. Had it come to deciding between Kennedy and Humphrey, the bosses would have been torn, but they weren't in the least torn when it came to deciding between McCarthy and Humphrey. To the shock and outrage of those Democrats who had supported McCarthy or Kennedy because of opposition to the war, the vice president, Lyndon Johnson's man, was handed the nomination on the first ballot.

Three kinds of Democrat fight for party dominance

Humphrey was narrowly defeated by Nixon in November, and in the aftermath of the election, the national Democratic Party, acting through the so-called McGovern Commission (nicknamed for its chair, U.S. Sen. George McGovern of South Dakota), concluded that the presidential nomination process could no longer be a boss-dominated thing. Rank-and-file Democrats would have to be given a voice, a very strong voice. In practice this meant that every state, not just a handful, would have to hold presidential primaries. The first experiment with this new system came in 1972, and the nominee produced by the process was none other than McGovern himself, the weakest presidential candidate in the long history of the Democratic Party. Nixon trounced him that November, in a landslide comparable to the FDR triumph over Alf Landon in 1936. Landon had lost every state but Maine and Vermont; McGovern won only a single state, Massachusetts, plus the District of Columbia.

This electoral disaster must have led many residents of the Aged Political Bosses Retirement Home to reflect that things worked better in the old days, when the machine-driven system produced winning candidates such as Franklin Roosevelt and John Kennedy. But from the reformers themselves the election outcome provoked no call for a return to the old machine-dominated system. Although they regretted that their man, McGovern, had not been elected, and although they continued to hate the man who *had* been elected (a hatred that bore fruit in the Watergate Crisis of 1973-1974), on the whole they were satisfied with the way things had worked out. The power of machines and bosses in the presidential selection process was now broken; the party had nominated a candidate who, although unpopular with the nation as a whole, including many Democratic voters, was (apart from the fact that he was badly defeated) very much to the liking of the reformers; and the reformers themselves had become important players in the national Democratic Party.

Had they been badly beaten in November? Sure — but so what? There would be other elections in the future, and the reform constituency would play an important role in these elections. In Democratic presidential primaries, the reformer types would play a role greatly disproportionate to their numbers because the new primary system favored political enthusiasts over lukewarm voters (since the latter usually don't bother going to the polls on primary day). And it favored energetic activists and organizers, especially if they had money behind them, over the waning powers of the political machines.

The years between 1968 (when Humphrey lost narrowly to Nixon) and 1972 (when McGovern lost overwhelmingly to Nixon) witnessed a dramatic change in the nature of the national Democratic Party. We can see clearly now that three distinct kinds of liberals were battling for control of it.

- *FDR liberals*. There were the old liberals of the New Deal variety, who had always been focused on the interests of working-class people generally and of union workers in particular. A great proportion of these New Deal liberals were themselves labor-union leaders. (By 1970 the New Deal might better have been called the Old Deal, so politically ancient was it by that date.)

• *Civil-rights liberals*. Then there were the liberals of the black civil-rights movement: blacks and their white sympathizers who held that the most pressing domestic problem of the day was the long and shameful American heritage of anti-black racism that went back through Jim Crow and slavery to the early decades of the seventeenth century. Thanks especially to Martin Luther King in the field and to Lyndon Johnson in the White House, these liberals had won two great and decisive political victories in the 1960s: the Civil Rights Act of 1964 and the Voting Rights Act of 1965. In the summers of 1967 and 1968 great riots took place in the black ghettos of many of the nation's big cities. Although this second class of liberals had nothing directly to do with initiating the riots, many of them expressed a certain degree of sympathy for the rioters, half-condoning their conduct by describing them as "protesters" against racism and oppression. These liberals, having won legal recognition for the principle of non-discrimination, were now pushing for something more, for something that would come to be called "affirmative action," consisting in a kind of positive discrimination or "preferential treatment" in favor of blacks to rectify America's long historical record of racial injustice.

• *Moral/cultural liberals*. "Moral" or "cultural" liberals (I use the terms interchangeably), who were for the most part enthusiastic supporters of the McGovern candidacy, had come of age during the cultural revolution of the 1960s. An important subdivision of the cultural revolution, as everyone knows, was the sexual revolution. Moral liberals were especially concerned with issues of individual freedom — in particular, sexual freedom. Most of their sexual-freedom battles were conducted outside the arena of politics — challenging old-fashioned sexual morality on college campuses, in the world of publishing, in the entertainment industry, and in the liberal churches.

Then there was the question of abortion. According to the ideology of moral liberalism, the legal and moral right to abortion was an absolutely essential thing. Moral liberals placed a tremendous emphasis on the value of personal autonomy — which had to include sexual freedom; otherwise, as they saw it, it would be a thin and watery autonomy. And for sexual freedom to be complete, abortion would be needed as a backup remedy whenever "mistakes" were made. Moreover, according to the ideal of autonomy, a woman was entitled to control her own body; what kind of control would she have if she were not free to expel unwanted fetuses from her uterus? Quite logically, then, moral liberals fought to get abortion laws liberalized by state legislatures, and in some states (e.g., New York and California) they had notable successes. But their greatest success came, not at the state level and not in legislative assemblies, but in the U.S. Supreme Court. In January 1973, only two months after McGovern's ignominious defeat, the Supreme Court handed down its famous (or notorious) *Roe v. Wade* ruling, which declared abortion a constitutionally protected right, and struck down almost every restrictive abortion law in the land.

Moral liberals were also semi-pacifist. To a great extent, this attitude was the result of their virtually unanimous opposition to the

Vietnam War, a view that had a tendency to expand into opposition to war in general. But it was also the result of their fundamental belief: the belief in the value of personal freedom. The logic went something like this: Personal freedom is good; hence, its opposite, coercion or compulsion, is bad. The military is a hierarchical system based on compulsion; hence, there's something intrinsically bad about the military. The most extreme form of compulsion is violence; hence, violence is especially bad. And warfare is the most extreme form of violence; hence, it's hard to imagine anything worse than war.

Both the pro-sex and the anti-war attitudes of the moral liberals, then, had the same philosophical root: the idea that personal liberty is the supreme good. These attitudes were neatly summed up in an expression that became popular during the Cultural Revolution: "Make love, not war" — which, translated into plain English, meant, "Practice sexual freedom, and oppose the military."

But moral liberals were normally, as I said, no more than "semi-pacifists." We can't describe them as total pacifists, for they conceded that some wars might be justified — the Civil War, for example, and World War II. Wars against slaveholders and Nazis, both of them egregious enemies of personal liberty and great perpetrators of violence, were morally permissible. And most moral liberals were willing to concede in the abstract that in the future there might be wars that would be justified. (Many supported the U.S. invasion of Afghanistan following 9/11, for instance.) Since they tend to be only semi-pacifists, most liberals don't call for complete abolition of the military. Instead they seek cuts in the Pentagon budget, a halt to the development of a "Star Wars" missile defense shield, and an end to military recruiting on college and university campuses.

Demise of the Political Machines

The great question facing the Democratic Party in the 1970s was this: Could these three varieties of liberalism — New Deal liberalism, civil-rights liberalism, and moral/cultural liberalism — combine to form a new Democratic coalition? The answer at the end of the day proved to be yes — but it was far from an easy answer to arrive at. For a long time the rank and file of the labor movement, made up almost entirely of white male blue-collar workers, was, to put it mildly, less than enthusiastic about the upward-mobility aspirations of blacks. Equality for blacks would mean that whites would have to compete with them for union jobs and the things, such as housing, that could be purchased with the wages of union jobs. But the top leadership of the unions — especially Walter Reuther, head of the United Auto Workers, who had also been the head of the CIO when the merger of the CIO and the AFL was accomplished in 1955 — saw that black and white workers had much in common, and the leadership gradually persuaded the rank and file to support the ideal of social and legal equality for blacks. By the early 1970s this black-white labor coalition had largely been achieved.

But could this two-part coalition be expanded by taking in a third member, the cultural/moral liberals? This looked as if it would be far more difficult, since the moral liberals came on average from a much higher step on the socioeconomic scale than did blacks or union workers; and the moral liberals had as an ideology — maximizing personal liberty, especially sexual liberty — something the other two groups had little interest in.[11] Indeed, the

[11] I don't mean to say that members of the other two groups were champions of chastity. Far from it. But they were

McGovern campaign of 1972 did little to encourage the hope that the three-part coalition could be achieved. After McGovern, the favorite of moral liberals, had won the Democratic nomination, many old-line Democratic politicians plus many union leaders — including most notably George Meany, head of the AFL-CIO — sat on their hands during the months leading up to the November election. This inaction contributed significantly to the dimensions of the McGovern defeat.

After the 1972 election, however, it became clear that these new liberals, the moral liberals, were not about to go away. No matter how much their presence displeased others, the pro-choicers, sexual liberationists, and semi-pacifists had won a place in the party. They had nominated a presidential candidate, and as long as the new presidential primary system remained in place, they could probably nominate further candidates. In the meantime, the White House was in the hands of a man, Richard Nixon, who would qualify as an anti-liberal from the point of view of all three species of liberalism; the three factions could unite in their hatred of Nixon — an important step toward forging the tripartite coalition. Gradually, then, the political division was healed (a striking example of the old proverb that politics makes for strange bedfellows), and by the 1980s the new Democratic coalition was firmly in place. There was, of course, considerable overlap among the three circles. Many in the union movement were sympathetic

usually conservative and conventional in their moral and religious beliefs, even if in practice they often deviated from them. It's one thing to take an illicit tumble in the hay; it's quite something else to become a crusader for sexual license.

to the civil-rights movement, and vice versa. Most cultural liberals, filled with a spirit of *noblesse oblige*, had a certain amount of sympathy for the labor movement. And more important, they felt a *very* strong sympathy with the civil-rights movement.

This latter sympathy was all the greater due to the fact that moral liberals interpreted the civil-rights movement in a way that served to enhance the legitimacy of their own newer brand of liberalism. The civil-rights movement embodied two traditional American values: freedom and equality. But which of the two was more important? Which was more characteristic of the movement? Old liberals of the New Deal type, for whom social equality for the working class was a central value, tended to see the civil-rights movement as mainly an equality movement. President Lyndon Johnson, himself a New Deal liberal if ever there was one, saw it this way. For Johnson, as he indicated in his famous Howard University commencement address of June 1965, achieving freedom by breaking the chains of the Jim Crow system was only a first step; next had to come the really important thing: the achievement of true social and economic equality between the races.

Moral liberals, however, didn't see the civil-rights movement as primarily an egalitarian drive. For them it was principally a movement of *liberation*. Blacks, as this new species of liberalism saw things, were freeing themselves from the bonds of racism in much the same way as moral liberals were freeing themselves from the bonds of conventional morality and sexual repression. Moral liberals saw a continuum, stretching from blacks at one end (who were first on the battlefield, having risen against their oppressors beginning at Montgomery, Alabama, in 1955) to homosexuals at the other (who didn't rise against their oppressors until the Greenwich Village "Stonewall" riots of 1969), with sexually liberated straight people (who rose up against the oppression of Puritanism in the early to mid-1960s) someplace in the middle. All three groups were struggling to throw off customary bonds of oppression and intolerance. To this day, three decades later, moral liberals still view the black civil-rights movement as a liberation movement and therefore as a precedent for sexual liberation, now including same-sex marriage. And there are more than a few prominent blacks, including the late widow of Martin Luther King, who have gone along with this interpretation, although it's doubtful that most rank-and-file African-Americans agree.

A new paradigm: from wealth to race

There was yet another way in which, by embracing (or co-opting) the black civil-rights movement, moral liberals advanced their cause and increased their strength within the Democratic Party. They intuitively understood that they'd be better situated politically if the central conflict in American politics were no longer the traditional conflict based on wealth, but one based on race.

From the first presidential candidacy of William Jennings Bryan in 1896, through the beginning of the New Deal in 1933, until about 1960, the great conflict in American politics was between the Haves and the Have-nots, the rich and the non-rich. The Republican Party represented the rich, the Democratic Party the non-rich. There were occasional exceptions to this partisan rule: some Republicans (Theodore Roosevelt, for example) expressed rather an un-Republican sympathy for the non-rich, while many conservative Democrats had a tender regard for the interests of the rich. But by and large, the fight between the two parties was a fight between the party of the rich (Republicans) and the party of the non-rich (Democrats).

The civil rights movement of the 1950s and '60s brought about a paradigm shift in American politics. No longer was the pivotal struggle between rich and non-rich. Now it was between blacks (in company with many non-racist white allies) and racist whites. This provided a wonderful political opening for affluent liberals; at least it did so when, during the Kennedy and Johnson administrations, the Democratic Party embraced the cause of the blacks. Hitherto it had been anything but easy for affluent persons to be Democrats, for the Democratic Party — working according to the class-conflict paradigm — was perceived as being opposed to the economic interests of the well-to-do. If you were a rich person, you would have to be willing to work against the economic interests of your social class. Some rich people, of course, were willing to do this (Franklin Roosevelt and John Kennedy, to name two of the most obvious), but the overwhelming majority of them were not.

The civil-rights movement suddenly changed this. If you were rich, you could now support the Democratic Party without shocking or outraging your friends and associates; they would see you as a believer in racial justice, not as a "traitor to your class" (the way many Republicans saw FDR). And the Democrats themselves, who might previously have been a bit suspicious of rich persons in their ranks, were now much more ready to welcome you. You were no longer an enemy simply by virtue of your wealth. And if enough people like you entered the Democratic ranks, the party might well reverse, or at least soften, its hostility toward the rich. Thus it was that in the 1960s there commenced the in-flowing of the rich, the near-rich, and the would-be-rich to the ranks of the Democratic Party. Since that era, the old anti-rich prejudice that used to be common among Democrats has gone into steep decline, and the national party — especially during the administration of President Bill Clinton — became a much more pro-business party than before. On the whole, it's true that rich (along with near-rich and would-be-rich) people today still prefer the Republican Party to the Democrats, but the preference isn't nearly as lopsided as it was in the days of FDR.

This has produced a weird configuration of American politics. If (using the terminology Aristotle uses in his *Politics*) we call the party of the rich the "oligarchic" party and the party of the non-rich the "democratic" party, then the United States today has one strongly oligarchic party (the Republicans), one moderately oligarchic party (the Democrats), and no truly democratic party. Having carried to completion a process that began in the 1960s, today's Democratic Party has ceased to be a genuinely democratic party. No wonder so many people toward the lower end of the socioeconomic scale don't bother to vote in elections; for they have no party that clearly represents their economic interests. And no wonder many toward the lower end who *do* vote often vote Republican. It isn't as if the Republicans will do a good job at taking care of the economic interests of these people; but neither, very probably, will the Democrats; and at least the Republicans promise to take care of many of their moral and cultural concerns.

The fact that this shift — from a class-conflict to a race-conflict paradigm — provides "cover" for rich and near-rich Democrats helps to explain a very curious phenomenon: many affluent Democrats, especially Democrats of the liberal intellectual variety (college professors and administrators, journalists at major news outlets, lawyers) continue to insist that the United States is a seriously racist nation, when it should seem perfectly clear that the back of American racism has long since been broken. If we make a distinction between race prejudice (a feeling or attitude) and race discrimination (behavior or conduct), we can concede that the former is still relatively widespread — although not nearly as widespread as it was a half-century ago — but the latter has largely disappeared from everyday American life. Race prejudice today is largely confined to whites of lower social standing; and much of it, it should be noted, isn't so much anti-black feeling as it is *anti-poor* feeling that gets directed at blacks because of their disproportionate poverty and because of the extremely unfortunate public image — reinforced by the entertainment industry, including its black-controlled sectors — that represents blacks as being poor, boorish, and criminal.

But among whites on the higher rungs of the socioeconomic ladder, there's very little anti-black feeling; and if these high-status whites object to certain poor people who happen to be black, they, unlike many lower-class whites, are able to distinguish between blackness and poverty.[12] These high-status whites are the Americans with real social and economic power, the ones who, if they wanted to, would be able to block the upward mobility of blacks in schools and the workplace; but so far from wanting to keep blacks "in their place," they typically want blacks to move up in the world, and they're willing to give blacks the benefit of the doubt when it comes to schooling and employment.

Among these powerful whites — persons who occupy high positions in the professions, in business, in higher education, in

[12] Two college professors, friends of mine, one of them white and the other black, one day had an argument. The black professor said accusingly to the white, "You don't like me because of the color of my skin." The white professor, very much a liberal, replied, "It has nothing to do with your skin. I don't like you because you're a pain in the ass."

public-school systems, and in government — race discrimination is minimal, not just because it's forbidden by the law, but because it's forbidden as well by the moral code generally accepted among persons of their lofty socioeconomic status. Further, these people are pro-black out of patriotic motives: they clearly understand that the United States will be better off if African-Americans, instead of being marginalized, as they have traditionally been, are fully "included" in American society.

Martin Luther King was one of the great figures in American history. Forty years ago, he (with many helpers, to be sure) persuaded the people of the United States to examine their collective conscience. They did, and they concluded that racism is a great sin — un-Christian, un-American, harmful to society, and just plain wrong. Yet despite this moral revolution, the myth persists among affluent moral liberals that racism is still a major problem in America. It's easy to understand why many black political leaders — or more accurately, many black political demagogues — would wish to perpetuate the myth. After all, their careers, which have been built upon doing bad imitations of Dr. King, depend on it. If the monster of white racism were truly crushed, they would be rendered obsolete — or worse, forced to confront the far more serious problems plaguing the black subculture today.

So much for black demagogues. But what motive do affluent whites have for perpetuating the racism myth? A twofold motive. For one, it allows them to think of themselves as morally superior to the great majority of their fellow-citizens. Were they in the habit of praying, they would offer a prayer of thanksgiving: "Thank you, Lord, for making me virtuous, so unlike those sinners who surround me in this hopelessly racist nation." For another, it allows them to have a good conscience about being so much more well-off economically than most of their fellow Americans. If the central political conflict in America were a struggle between the rich and the non-rich, these affluent liberals would feel embarrassed and perhaps slightly ashamed or guilty at their economic good fortune. But if the crucial conflict is between racists and anti-racists, there's no need to feel uncomfortable about having lots of money. For these affluent liberals are on the side of the angels, the anti-racist side. They might not be black themselves, but they're the next best thing: whites who have profound sympathy for their oppressed black brothers and sisters. As long as racism, not economic inequality, remains the central issue in American political life, today's Democratic Party — the ostentatiously anti-racism party — will be the natural home of affluent moral liberals.

From race to sex

The position of moral/cultural liberals in the Democratic Party was further strengthened by the rise of feminism, which took place at the same time as the rise of the new liberalism, in the mid to late 1960s. A natural alliance between the two soon developed. In fact, it was more than an alliance: the two largely overlapped one another, and in the end feminism has become a subclass of moral/cultural liberalism.

If we're looking for a starting date for modern feminism,[13] the best year to choose is probably 1963, the year of the publication of Betty Friedan's bestseller, *The Feminine Mystique*. The feminist movement no doubt would have come about without Friedan's book, but the book, which had the good luck to come along at just

[13] I say "modern feminism" to distinguish it from the older era of American feminism that began in the 1830s and came to an end with the passage of the 19th Amendment (women's right to vote) in 1919.

the right moment, served as a trigger for setting off an explosion that would have taken place sooner or later. The feminist movement seemed to follow inevitably from the black civil-rights movement. If blacks are to be liberated from domination by whites, it was reasoned, why shouldn't women be liberated from domination by men?[14]

At first the focus of the feminist movement was on equality — equality of opportunity for women in education, government, business, the professions, and the like. To this day, more than forty years after the commencement of the modern feminism movement, equality remains an important theme. But almost from the beginning of the movement, freedom has also been an important theme — so much so that for many years feminism was routinely spoken of by non-feminists, as well as by some feminists, as the "women's liberation movement" ("women's lib"). Women were to be set free from what they saw as the oppression of men, the regime of *patriarchy* that had been in place for thousands and thousands of years. According to feminists of this liberationist stripe,[15] men (with a few exceptions here and there) are the enemy. Men are sexist the way whites are racist, and for much the same reason: just as whites profit from the enforced subordination of blacks in a

[14] This is similar to what had happened more than a century earlier, when the abolition movement led to the first women's movement. If black slaves should be free, reasoned the feminists of the 1830s and '40s, why shouldn't women — whose position in society, although not exactly slavish, bore a certain resemblance to the condition of slaves — also be free?

[15] Such feminists are often referred to by their critics as "radical feminists." Although in my view this isn't an inappropriate label, I'll refer to them here, less invidiously, by my own coinage of "liberation feminists."

racist regime, so males profit from the enforced subordination of women in a sexist regime.

One of the most important forms of sexist subordination has to do with sexuality. According to the liberation feminists, men have always wished to control the sexuality of women by restricting and repressing it. From this wish followed the traditional emphasis on premarital virginity for women, along with the traditional sexual double standard: what was sauce for the goose was definitely *not* sauce for the gander. What also followed from this patriarchal idea of women, according to liberation feminists, was the supposedly traditional idea that there's something indecent about a woman, even a married woman, who enjoys sex.[16] Working from this premise, liberation feminists saw other elements of a patriarchal conspiracy in certain laws (enacted, of course, by patriarchal male lawmakers) that remained on the books until relatively recent times: laws to prohibit the manufacture and sale of contraceptives,

[16] At first glance, this seems one of the weirdest ideas held by feminists — namely, that men prefer having sex with women who don't enjoy sex. But this idea makes perfect sense once it's realized that for a man to have sex with a woman who doesn't enjoy the act is something like rape: the man is in effect saying to his wife, "I know you don't want to do this, but I'm your master, so I'm going to make you do it anyway." If you believe, as many liberation feminists did (and still do), that the sexual relationship between husband and wife is a milder version of the sexual relationship between rapist and victim, and that the satisfaction the husband gets out of the sex act is not so much sexual gratification as gratification of a will to power, then you can also believe that a man prefers having sex with a wife who views sexual intercourse as an unpleasant but necessary burden, something like washing the laundry or cleaning the floor.

laws that made it difficult for a woman to divorce her oppressive husband, and laws that prohibited abortion.

If women were to be liberated, according to liberation feminism, they must first of all be liberated in their sexuality. The ideal of premarital virginity must be done away with, as must the sexual double standard generally. Women must come to understand that sexual desire and satisfaction are as normal for them as for men, and they must put this understanding into practice. They must be free to divorce husbands they find unsatisfactory and to find new husbands or new lovers. And it was absolutely indispensable that contraception and abortion be readily available: for how can women control their sexual lives when there's a risk of unwanted pregnancy or when, such pregnancies occurring, there's no way to terminate them?

A still more complete way of keeping men from controlling the sexual lives of women might be for women to be lesbian or at least bisexual. Some liberation feminists actually argued that lesbianism made for a more authentic and reliable brand of feminist.[17] The logical conclusion from this was that if you wanted to be a true feminist, you ought to enter into a lesbian relationship. Most feminists, it turns out, were unwilling or unable to go down this

[17] An example of this can be found in Martha Shelley's "Notes of a Radical Lesbian," an essay that appeared in the 1970 book *Sisterhood Is Powerful*, a liberation-feminist anthology whose unifying theme is the idea of oppressive patriarchy. According to Shelley, "A woman who is totally independent of men — who obtains love, sex, and self-esteem from other women — is a terrible threat to male supremacy. . . . If hostility to men causes Lesbianism, then it seems to me that in a male-dominated society, Lesbianism is a sign of mental health" (Robin Morgan, ed., *Sisterhood Is Powerful* [New York: Vintage Press, 1970], 308).

road. But they did the next best thing: they honored lesbians and lesbianism and did battle for the civil rights of lesbians. But since the rights of lesbians were part and parcel of the rights of homosexuals generally, the feminist fight for lesbian rights became a fight for homosexual rights in general.

Supporting gay men was a very different thing from supporting heterosexual men (i.e., patriarchal oppressors), for gay men by their very nature have no wish to dominate women or to control their sexuality. Besides, gay men have been oppressed by the very same people who have traditionally oppressed women — heterosexual males. And they've been oppressed, worse still, because they reminded heterosexual males of women: gays seemed to these males to be unmanly men, womanish men. If women were to be held in contempt as an inferior kind of being, gay men would have to be held in similar contempt. From this it followed that the liberation of women and the liberation of gay men were inextricably linked to one another. So at least the liberation feminists came to think.

Although feminists have always come in both varieties — equality feminists and liberation feminists (not to mention the kind of feminist who evenly balanced the two themes) — it was liberation feminism that eventually came to dominate the feminist movement. A striking illustration of this was given during the Lewinsky-Clinton scandal of 1998. From the point of view of equality feminism, which is preoccupied with male-female inequality in the workplace, Clinton's treatment of Monica Lewinsky was outrageous. Even if Lewinsky's participation was seemingly voluntary, there is inevitably, egalitarian feminists had hitherto insisted, an element of involuntariness when a male boss (and such a powerful boss in this case!) wants sex from a female subordinate. But did the feminist establishment lament this sexual exploitation? Hardly a peep of protest came from them.

What a contrast to what had happened a few years earlier when, during the Supreme Court nomination hearings for Clarence Thomas, Anita Hill came forward and avowed that Thomas, when he was her boss, had . . . done what? Raped her? Demanded that she go to bed with him? Received sexual favors, as Clinton had done? Not at all. His alleged crime was that *he had talked dirty to her* a few times after hours. Yet it caused an earthquake. This was the occasion, remember, when that feminist among feminists, Rep. Pat Schroeder of Colorado, led a contingent of women members of the U.S. House on a short but very public march from the House side to the Senate side of the Capitol, chanting that men "still don't get it."

What was the true difference, from the feminist point of view, between the Clinton and the Thomas cases? It had to do with abortion. Thomas was strongly suspected (and rightly suspected, as it turned out) of disagreeing with the ruling in *Roe v. Wade*. Thomas, in other words, was the enemy of "a woman's right to choose." But the right to abortion is one of the central values of liberation feminism; indeed it's the crucial value, since, if the right to abortion were to be abolished, the sexual-liberation dominoes would all fall. So Thomas's minor sins (if in fact he committed them) had to be treated like major felonies. Clinton, on the other hand, had given unstinting support to the abortion-rights cause. His support was most convincingly demonstrated when he twice (in 1996 and 1997) vetoed bills that would have banned partial-birth abortion, a procedure that's hardly distinguishable from outright infanticide. Since the president was so loyally committed to a central tenet of liberation feminism, he could easily be forgiven a little bit of sexual exploitation in the workplace. Besides, only an equality feminist would have a problem with it in the first place. Lewinsky was a consenting adult, wasn't she? Like a good liberated woman, she was simply expressing her sexuality in the manner of her choosing.

It was easy, then, for moral/cultural liberalism to make an alliance with liberation feminism, since they believed in the same things. Indeed they were very much the same people. If you were a cultural liberal, you were almost certainly also a liberation feminist, and if you were a liberation feminist, you were almost certainly a cultural liberal too. Both subscribed to the two central tenets of moral liberalism:

- The *Personal Liberty Principle*, or PLP, which says you're free to do whatever you want, provided you don't hurt non-consenting others in a direct, obvious, immediate, and tangible way.

- The *Tolerance Principle*, which says you must tolerate the conduct of others, provided they don't hurt non-consenting others in a direct, obvious, immediate, and tangible way.

Both cultural liberals and liberation feminists were also secularists: predominantly agnostic or atheistic in personal belief, hostile toward organized religion in general and traditional Christianity in particular, and committed to replacing traditional Christian morality with moral liberalism. The only difference between the generic cultural liberal and the liberation feminist was that the former favored liberation for everyone, while the latter, although not being opposed to universal liberation, had a special focus on the liberation of women. Once the feminist movement was largely taken over by its liberation wing, the natural alliance was consummated, and feminism became a department of cultural liberalism.

Incorporating the feminist movement within the moral/cultural liberalism movement greatly enhanced the power of the latter within the national Democratic Party, for cultural liberalism, thanks to its merger with feminism, could now assert of itself what the feminist movement had always asserted: that it was the authentic and authoritative voice of all American women. Of course, this claim was not correct, since many women had always been opposed to feminism, and even more women were opposed to the liberation variety of feminism. But in the first decade or so of feminism (dating the movement from Betty Friedan's 1963 book), the feminist claim to speak for *all* women had a certain plausibility. The feminist drive for equality and freedom looked like a cultural tidal wave that would eventually sweep all the old landmarks away. Everyone knew that *some* women didn't like the new feminism and its ideals, but these were thought to be old women or uneducated women — just the ones you'd expect to be the last people to appreciate a good new idea; the same people who would be the last to use ATMs or cell phones. Sooner or later, the old women would die off, and eventually the enlightened new ideas on women would trickle down to the less-educated. If the feminist movement didn't speak for all women at the moment, it would speak, it seemed, for all women at a rapidly arriving future moment. And so the feminist/cultural liberal claim to speak for all women was widely accepted — especially by the press.

In the 1970s, then, it *seemed* that cultural liberals (including feminists) spoke for *all* American women, plus many American men. So how could the Democratic Party do anything but welcome them into the house? Even if the few remaining urban political bosses and old-school labor leaders didn't like the cultural liberals, so what? They were now too powerful to be disregarded. There were too many of them to be ignored. They'd have to be granted a seat at the table; a place in the three-part liberal coalition that the Democratic Party had now undeniably become.

Chapter 2

The Great Transformation, Part 2: Rise of the Ideologues

In the preceding chapter, we distinguished between two great eras in the history of the Democratic Party: an earlier era in which local and state political machines played a major role in the life of the national party; and the present era (commencing in the early 1970s), in which the machines play little or no role.

As it so happened, it was precisely at this moment of transition that I became a Democratic politician. I had no sympathy for the old boss-led political machines, and so I naturally joined with the reformers. Eventually, as it turned out, I also lost all sympathy with the reformers, who today dominate the Democratic Party.

It was the Vietnam War that ignited my career in politics. At the beginning I had been a supporter of the war, largely because it was a Lyndon Johnson undertaking, and I was a great fan of President Johnson. I saw him as a kind of second coming of Franklin Roosevelt, in that from the time of his first State of the Union Address in 1964, he made it clear that he intended to use the immense power of the federal government to improve the life conditions of those at the lower end of America's socioeconomic ladder. This was a very FDR-ish thing to do. And in one very important respect, LBJ was willing to go even further than Roosevelt had gone. FDR had moved very cautiously, to say the least, when it came to equal treatment for black Americans. His wife might have been an earnest egalitarian on race, but Roosevelt had to govern the country and win the war, which meant retaining the support of senators and congressmen from the white-supremacist South. But by the time Johnson came to the White House, the political situation had grown more favorable for a president to become a strong champion of equality for blacks, and in the end, Johnson proved to be the best White House friend to African-Americans since Lincoln.

In 1964, using the prestige of the presidency and the skills he had honed while majority leader of the Senate, Johnson won passage of a landmark Civil Rights Act. And in 1965, following the shocking incidents at Selma, Alabama, he delivered his great "We shall overcome" address to Congress, the initial step toward winning passage a few months later of the Voting Rights Act. This latter, which assured a general right to vote for blacks for the first time since the end of Reconstruction (1877), transformed the political landscape of the South. Johnson prophesied, quite correctly as it turned out, that the act would drive many southern Democrats out of the party, but he went ahead nonetheless, putting humanity and patriotism above narrower political interests.

How could I, with my old-school Democratic (and Catholic) social conscience, not admire LBJ? And so, when he decided to go into Vietnam in a big way in 1965, I was more than ready to give him the benefit of the doubt. When people told me that the war was a great mistake (a conclusion I was eventually to reach myself), my response in effect was this: "Johnson has been right on everything else, so he is very probably right on this too."[18] I also believed that the United States could not permit expansion of the Communist "empire." In the interests of peaceful co-existence, the Communists, as middle-of-the-road Americans generally saw things, could keep what they had already won, but they mustn't be allowed to take more. That had been our principle in responding to the Berlin blockade of the late '40s, and it was our principle again when North Korea invaded South Korea in 1950. This geopolitical policy seemed to me to be a wise one, and if, in pursuit of it, President Johnson now thought that we should make a large commitment of American troops, well, that was fine with me.

But time, along with much public criticism of the war and an apparent lack of American success, eventually changed my mind. I came to see that North Vietnam was not part of a monolithic Communist empire. Its Communism was home-grown — like Yugoslavia's — not imposed from outside. We could expect, then, that like Yugoslavia it would pursue an independent policy; it would not be a puppet of China or the Soviet Union; in fact, it might even, again like Yugoslavia, prove to be thorn in the side of Russia or China or both. Hence, a Communist victory in the South would be no great threat to the interests of the United States. Compounding my disillusionment was my conclusion that

[18] The problem was this: Johnson had a profound understanding of American domestic realities, and therefore could rely on his own judgment when it came to domestic social policies. But he knew little about foreign affairs, and therefore had to rely on the advice of others. And so his near-infallibility in the one realm deserted him when he moved to the other. This distinction, I believe, was first noted by John Kenneth Galbraith in his review of Johnson's book of memoirs.

Johnson — my hero — had lied to the country in order to bolster support for the war. The better part of valor, I finally judged sometime in 1967, would be to cut our losses and leave, allowing Communist North Vietnam to prevail.

My opposition to the war, I should note, wasn't motivated by any fear that I might be drafted. By 1965, the year Johnson decided to make a big commitment of American troops, I was twenty-seven and no longer draft-eligible. Nor did I have any sympathy, sneaking or otherwise, for the Communist regime of North Vietnam. In those days (when I happened to be living in Boston, teaching at a small Catholic women's college), it was easy to meet young people who believed that the government of North Vietnam was "progressive" and the government of the United States just a little short of fascist. But I wasn't a member of the Jane Fonda brigade. My anti-Communist sentiments went back to the time when the Cold War began, in the late 1940s — I was less than ten years old when I began absorbing patriotic anti-Red propaganda — and had only grown stronger over the years as I had become aware of the disastrous consequences of Communist ideas.

No, I simply came to see our involvement in Vietnam as without purpose or benefit, moral or political — one of the great policy mistakes in American history, a real political tragedy. In fact, I think this more than ever today. For not only was it a needless war, but it contributed mightily to the great American cultural revolution of the 1960s and '70s — the essence of which (as I've argued elsewhere[19]) was a generalized rebellion against authority. This cultural revolution, I contend, has served to elevate the place of secularism in American culture and to depress the place

[19] See my book *The Decline and Fall of the Catholic Church in America*, especially chapters 4 through 8.

of Christianity generally and of Catholicism in particular. At the time of the war, I could see that it was very harmful to my country; what I couldn't see at the time was that it would also prove harmful to my party and my Church.

In November of 1967, Sen. Eugene McCarthy (a Catholic — and not just a Catholic but, unlike the vast majority of Catholic politicians, a theologically sophisticated one) announced that he would be entering the Democratic presidential primaries of 1968, running against Lyndon Johnson as an anti-war candidate. As the date for the first primary drew near, my wife, Maureen, and I paid a weekend visit to New Hampshire so that we could get a close-up view of the candidates. One evening we stopped for a drink at a hotel frequented by many campaign workers, and Allard Lowenstein approached our table. He didn't bother introducing himself, but he didn't need to. We knew who he was: the New York liberal activist who had persuaded McCarthy to enter the race (after having been rejected by Sen. Robert Kennedy). Lowenstein talked briefly with us, discovered we were spectators only, and urged us to get involved in the McCarthy campaign. And when we returned to Rhode Island, we did exactly that — although our efforts failed to convince the state Democratic committee to send even a single McCarthy delegate to the nominating convention.

In the interval between Bobby Kennedy's death and the meeting of the convention in August, Lowenstein convened a meeting at Chicago to call for the McCarthy and Kennedy people to work together in hopes of bringing about an "open convention" (translated into English, this meant "a convention that will choose an anti-war candidate" — in other words, anybody but Humphrey). I attended the gathering, and with a number of others, I one day witnessed a hallway debate between Lowenstein's wife and the famous CBS reporter Mike Wallace. Mrs. Lowenstein was deploring the fact that the Democratic Party in New York state,[20] made up of officials who had been elected to their party posts a few years earlier, had just chosen its delegation to the Democratic National Convention without paying any attention to the current state of Democratic public opinion about the war; in other words, they elected a delegation that didn't meet with the approval of Mr. and Mrs. Lowenstein or of any of the rest of us anti-war Democrats who had gathered in Chicago. Wallace countered that if you wanted to control the choices of the New York Democratic Party, you should have run candidates for party office a few years earlier. She responded that this was impossible; for who knew at the time how people would feel now about the war? Wallace replied that this is how the democratic system works: if you want an effective voice, you have to take the trouble to participate in low-level elections; you can't just shout your demands and assume that those who *did* take the trouble to participate have an obligation to heed you.

Much though I admired Lowenstein and his wife, I thought Wallace had the better of the argument. In fact, his argument was similar to one I had already made to myself, as a result of which I had decided to enter a race for the Rhode Island State Senate. I had no patience with those critics of the war (and of racism, the other great *bête noire* of the era) who held that the "system" was broken and that political reform would have to be brought about by action in the "street." I believed what I've always believed, that

[20] It's worth noting that New York in those days was the most populous state; hence, it would be sending the largest delegation to the national convention.

we live in a genuine, functioning democracy and that the way to bring about progressive change is to participate in the democratic process at the electoral level. If you refuse to participate, don't blame others when things go wrong; blame yourself.

The "open convention" wing of the party was defeated at the Chicago National Democratic Convention of 1968, but eventually it was this wing — what I've called in the preceding chapter the moral-liberalism wing — that prevailed. Its profound unhappiness with the outcome of the convention might have contributed to Humphrey's narrow loss to Nixon in November (although I myself quite willingly voted for Humphrey, and urged others to do the same, as he was clearly, it seemed to me, the lesser of two evils). The great demand made by us open-convention folks after the election was that we must never again have a nomination process like that of 1968; in other words, the bosses should be taken out of the process and delegates should be chosen by voters in Democratic primaries. The McGovern Commission gave us what we wanted — and even if the first candidate it produced, McGovern himself in 1972, was trounced, after he was gone the forces that produced his candidacy remained.

At the time, I thought of these people as the good guys: good-government, anti-boss reformers who were bent on the benign task of making the party more democratic (small *d*) and more responsive to the party rank and file. I didn't realize that they harbored within themselves the potential for passionate commitments to abortion rights and same-sex marriage, and a deep hostility toward traditional Christianity. I knew, of course, that they were sympathetic to a revision of American abortion laws, but I thought that this was a preference that wouldn't flourish. After all, I reasoned, pro-abortion attitudes would be deeply offensive to Catholic voters, and the Democratic Party could ill afford to offend its old standby. Therefore, this pro-abortion attitude would soon enough be dropped; it would have to be, at least by anyone who wanted to take part in something more than armchair politics. How naive and ignorant I was.

So as we moved from one era of the party's history (the age of machines and bosses) into a new era (the age of moral-liberal ideologues), I was on the side of the ideologues — at least with regard to everything except abortion, to which I retained my old religious and philosophical objections. Little did I foresee the effects that the party's new power structure would produce. It would take me years — decades even — before I fully realized that I could no longer be on their side and that, indeed, I would have to become their enemy.

Ideology replaces party organization

In the earlier era, the national party was answerable to the local and state parties. The national party — including the president, when a Democrat happened to occupy the White House — had to pay careful attention to the ideas and wishes of the local and state parties.[21] If it did not, it risked paying a heavy price at the polls; the

[21] For an interesting and amusing illustration of this truth, see David McCullough's account, in chapter 8 of his book *Truman* (Simon and Schuster, 1992; 292-324), of how Sen. Harry S. Truman was given the Democratic nomination for vice president in 1944, at a moment when it seemed probable to many observers that Franklin Roosevelt wouldn't live long enough to complete a fourth term. FDR, it seems, would have preferred keeping Henry Wallace, his third-term VP, but a number of big-city bosses wanted to get rid of Wallace, and Truman seemed to them the best alternative. Roosevelt, despite being the most powerful president in American history, had little choice but to succumb to the wishes of the bosses.

national party couldn't afford to have the local bosses sit on their hands during an election season.

In the days before TV ads and other very pricey political advertising, the national party depended upon local parties to serve three important political functions: initiation, education, and mobilization.

- *Initiation*. Local parties brought citizens into the democratic political process, giving them their political "baptism" and enabling them to be full participants in the political life of society. This initiation was especially important for immigrants and the children of immigrants, for by turning these people into "political animals," the local parties were also speeding up their process of Americanization.

  The initiation was not a superficial or merely pro-forma thing. When the local party turned you into a Democrat, it did so in a more or less permanent way: you had very probably become a Democrat for life (hence the analogy with baptism, which turns a person into a Christian for life). This meant that the national party could rely on your vote in election after election. Every so often, you might vote against the candidate for mayor (out of disgust, for instance, at the latest corruption scandal), but you'd hardly dream of voting against the Democratic presidential candidate, and you'd rarely or never vote against the Democratic candidate for U.S. House or Senate. The "yellow-dog Democrat"[22] was an extreme example of this type of loyalist, but in a more moderate form the type was very common. When

[22] A Democrat who is so loyal to the party that he would cheerfully vote for a yellow dog if the Democrats nominated one.

both Republican and Democratic machines were in operation, the "swing voter" was a relatively rare thing.

• *Education*. Local parties instructed their people on the political issues of the day. This was, of course, a one-sided education — essentially partisan propaganda. But a one-sided education is better than no education at all, especially in an open society in which the other side is free to present its counterarguments. The result was that local voters had a relatively high degree of political literacy. The local party transmitted the chief messages of the national party to the Democratic voter, who would then be able to justify his vote for Franklin Roosevelt by noting that FDR stood for X, Y, and Z.

• *Mobilization*. Local parties turned out the vote on Election Day, reminding people of their duty to vote and in some cases virtually dragging them to the polls. The local voter-mobilization apparatus would guarantee that hardcore Democrats and their families got out to vote. Nobody would be allowed to forget what day it was, and few would be lazy enough to withstand the pressure to get out of the house and go to the polling place.

The slow disintegration of the local machines in the 1950s and '60s and their rapid collapse after that meant that the national party was no longer answerable to local parties — but by the same token, it could no longer rely on local parties to help win elections. A great vacuum was created. Now, it might be debatable as to whether "nature" abhors a vacuum, but without question politics does. How was the political vacuum filled? With big money and with ideologues; and both the big money and the ideologues came from a new class — new, at least, to the Democratic Party.

Without the machines to keep them in line at the local level, diehard party loyalists became rarer, and more and more swing voters appeared on the scene: people who prided themselves on being independent thinkers who "vote the man," not the party. In the previous era, party loyalists could pretty much be taken for granted without much maintenance: only routine upkeep was needed to make sure they would vote the party ticket time after time. The large and rapidly growing class of swing voters, by contrast, had to be persuaded and re-persuaded in election after election. So how was the national party to meet this new, greatly enhanced need for persuasion? Above all, by means of television ads. Beginning in the 1950s and increasing steadily since then, TV political advertising has come to play a gigantic role in presidential election campaigns — and not just in presidential campaigns but in any campaign in which the candidate has to reach a very large number of voters: campaigns for the U.S. House and Senate, for governor, or for mayor of a large city.

But TV advertising, as everyone knows, isn't cheap: production costs are high, and the cost of buying air time is even higher. So to be a viable candidate for these higher offices, you must be able to raise lots of money, and candidates for major office soon learned that it's far more important to cultivate donors — especially those key donors who will not only give generously themselves but will persuade others to give generously — than to cultivate local political parties. The latter could do little or nothing for you in the post-machine era, while the former could provide you with that absolutely indispensable thing: money for TV ads.

And where did this money come from? Mostly from affluent people, of course. Like the famous bank robber Willie Sutton, who said he robbed banks because "that's where the money is," politicians solicit contributions from people who have enough money to be able to afford to give some of it away. And why were affluent people giving big money to Democratic candidates? Often they had economic interests to protect: businessmen and "trial lawyers" (i.e., lawyers who represent plaintiffs in liability suits) have been generous contributors. But now the wealthy were beginning to donate to the Democratic Party for another reason: to protect and advance their ideological concerns — that is, the items on the agenda of moral liberalism.

The socioeconomic center of gravity of the Democratic Party was shifting. What had once been a predominantly blue-collar party was increasingly taking on an upper-middle-class coloration, as more and more upper- and upper-middle-class people were voting Democratic and, more important, were willing to give some of their money to Democratic candidates.

But it wasn't just the money that made people of this kind so attractive to and influential within the evolving party. These affluent moral liberals were also strategically situated in what may be called the three "command posts" of American culture: tending to dominate the national press (as reporters and editors), the nation's high-prestige colleges, universities, and law schools (as faculty and administration), and the entertainment industry (as performers, writers, and producers). Thus, they were in a position to influence public opinion — both the short-term public opinion about events of the day and the long-term public opinion that gives shape to American culture. The press and the entertainment industry especially impacted short-term opinion, while the professors especially impacted long-term opinion. To get these opinion-makers on the side of the national Democratic Party, it was clear, was vitally important for the party, especially with local machines no longer serving to educate/propagandize their voters.

And it wasn't difficult to get these opinion-makers on the Democratic side. From the 1930s and for many decades following, the American intellectual class was predominantly liberal (in one sense or another of that poly-significant word) and Democratic. In fact, liberals and Democrats had something approaching a monopoly in the world of American intellectuals. If you thought of yourself as an intellectual, your "default" political position was liberalism. For decades, beginning in the 1930s and running through the 1960s, the expressions "conservative intellectual" and "Republican intellectual" seemed to be almost self-contradictory.

So much was this the case, so little did it seem that conservative convictions could be based on good reasons, that many liberals felt that people who professed to be conservative must be suffering from some kind of psychopathology. This was one of the lessons liberals took from the very influential 1950 work *The Authoritarian Personality*, which argued, in what was an apparently very scientific manner, that persons with an "authoritarian" personality usually hold right-wing political views; these authoritarian types are potential fascists, having a psychological profile similar to that of Germans who ardently supported Hitler. Liberal intellectuals utilized this thesis to say that people who held right-wing political views had potentially fascist personalities. The most notorious result of this equation was a 1964 issue of *Psychology Today* in which a number of otherwise respectable psychologists gave their judgment that Barry Goldwater, the conservative Republican candidate for president that year, was mentally ill.

Beginning in the 1950s, of course, there were a few intellectual conservatives — Russell Kirk, William Buckley, Whittaker Chambers, and their epigones — but with very few exceptions the liberal intellectual world didn't take them seriously. Buckley caught the attention of the liberal intellectuals, alternatively amusing and irritating them, but only rarely did he cause them to re-examine their principles or to doubt their conviction that they possessed the truth about political and social justice; and so the intellectual world remained overwhelmingly liberal in its politics during the 1950s and '60s.

Beginning in the mid-1960s, however, the class of conservative intellectuals significantly expanded. Added to the "old" conservatives of the Buckley-Kirk-Chambers variety were the neoconservatives, former New Deal and civil-rights liberals who had grown disillusioned by the emerging moral liberalism and semi-pacifism of the younger generation of liberals. Many older liberals (Norman Podhoretz, then editor of *Commentary* magazine, and his wife, Midge Decter, were striking examples of the type) were shocked and offended by student radicals, whom they regarded as un-patriotic and un-intellectual, if not downright anti-intellectual, and as promoting a very dubious personal ethic. With these new recruits came greater intellectual prestige for conservatism. But not enough prestige — for even today liberalism (and, of course, the Democratic Party) remains the default position for the young person who considers himself intellectually superior.

By and large, the occupants of America's cultural "command posts" — the press, the universities, the entertainment industry — like to think of themselves as intellectually superior persons, and so the great majority of them fall into the "default" position; they become liberals and Democrats. In this way America's intellectual class has become, on the whole, a marvelous resource for the national Democratic Party: a shaper of both short-term and long-term public opinion that can be mobilized — or more accurately, will self-mobilize — to promote the Democratic Party and the Democratic agenda.

But there was one hitch. Intellectuals are not attached to the Democratic Party the way Boston baseball fans are attached to the Red Sox. They don't say, "My party, right or wrong!" or, as the Red Sox fan might say, "The Sox, win or lose!" Intellectuals are people who, by definition, take ideas seriously, and America's liberal intellectuals remain loyal to the Democratic Party only as far as the Democratic agenda is favorable to their liberal beliefs and values. Let the party embrace more conservative beliefs and values — if, for example, the party were to abandon or moderate its strong support for abortion — and the liberal intellectual would soon jump ship. Fear of losing this support, I suggest, is one of the chief reasons that the big shots in the party aren't about to shift away from their abortion and same-sex-marriage positions.

This isn't to say that liberal intellectuals are such thoroughgoing ideologues that they'll never tolerate tactical deviations from the liberal agenda. They, like conservative intellectuals, understand that politics is the art of the possible. Thus, they appreciate that a certain amount of deviation might be necessary in order to win this legislative battle or that election. In recent campaigns, many politicians sympathetic to the secularist agenda have also claimed a personal religious devotion: they quote the Bible, wax eloquent on faith, reminisce about their former days singing in the church choir or serving at the altar. Now, for liberal intellectuals, bringing religion into politics is typically a no-no; however, these politicians can be forgiven their religious utterances, necessary as they are to undercut the many appeals to religion made by conservatives. Moral liberals understand that their agenda can be better carried out by leaders who are able to pass muster, in the eyes of voters, as personally religious. And they have no fear that this agenda will not be carried out: for despite their declarations of how much religion means to them in their personal life, these politicians invariably insist that their beliefs would not hinder their support for "a woman's right to choose" and other favored liberal causes.

Thus, liberal intellectuals can tolerate Democrats who make rhetorical deviations from the secularist playbook, provided these deviations contribute to the achievement of moral liberalism's long-term goals. That is, provided that the purpose of talking about faith or old-fashioned moral values is to snooker the general public, concealing the strategic advance of moral liberalism under a tactical fog of conservative-sounding language. But they can't tolerate Democrats who actually reject the distinctive values of moral liberalism: abortion rights, gay rights (including the right to same-sex marriage), the de-Christianization of the public square, and a semi-pacifist attitude toward foreign policy and the use of military force.

These were the terms of the bargain, then. If liberal intellectuals occupying the command posts of American culture were to aid the Democrats by generating pro-Democrat propaganda, Democrats in turn would have to aid the liberal intellectuals by promoting their cultural agenda. And so, beginning in the 1970s, the alliance was cemented, and the Democratic Party became the party of moral liberalism. The party didn't forget the other two members of the liberal coalition: New Deal liberalism, so dear to organized labor, and civil-rights liberalism, so dear to minorities, especially blacks. But more and more the liberalism that really counted was moral liberalism. For it was moral liberals who, in addition to providing the campaign funds that Democratic candidates needed in the age of TV advertising, could also provide the cultural influence the party craved.

Political Manichaeism

Since morally liberal intellectuals are ideologues, and since the Democratic Party came to rely on the support given by these intellectuals, it followed that the party was increasingly transformed into an ideological party. From slightly different causes, a similar transformation took place in the Republican Party, and the result is that American politics today, at least at the national level, is highly ideological. Combined with the demise of local machines, this has produced another phenomenon, which may be called political Manichaeism.

Manicheaism was a religious movement that flourished in the Roman Empire in the fourth and fifth centuries.[23] The religion blended elements of Christianity with elements of Persian dualism. The ancient Persian religion (commonly called Zoroastrianism) held that the universe is the product of a struggle between two great cosmic forces: the good force (light) and the evil force (darkness), thus explaining why our world is such a confused mix of good and evil and why we ourselves seem to be partly good, partly evil. The Manicheans identified the good force with spirit and the evil with matter; this meant that our souls were good but our bodies evil, and the moral life of a human being was a constant war between them.

[23] St. Augustine, before his conversion (or re-conversion) to Catholicism, was a Manichean, and his account of the movement, given in his *Confessions*, is well worth reading.

Ideological politics tends to become Manichean politics. That is, the contesting ideological parties tend to think of themselves as totally correct and hence purely good, and their enemies as totally incorrect and hence purely evil; and the more purely evil your enemy is, the more purely good you are, since you're the only force preventing the triumph of pure evil. Thus, in today's ideological American political landscape, ideological-Manichean Democrats regard the Religious Right and President George W. Bush as not just mistaken but positively *wicked.*[24] (The Republicans are no better. Consider the anger and hatred directed throughout his presidency at President Bill Clinton, culminating in 1998 in a needless and foolish impeachment.)

Current ideological politics isn't just Manichean — it's also increasingly *shrill*. As we've seen, in the absence of local machines, there are fewer reliable, dedicated partisans. Therefore both parties must make a greater effort, on the national level, to keep voters in their camp. The troops can never be allowed a prolonged rest period; they have to be continually rallied by a relentless stream of commercials, press releases, press conferences, TV interviews, talk-show commentary, and the like. At the same time, a decline in the party loyalty that the old machines did so much to sustain means that there are more "persuadables" floating around in the political world — independents along with semi-partisans not firmly attached to their parties — who also need to be piqued

[24] A nice (although somewhat tongue-in-cheek) illustration of this Manicheaism can be found in the title and subtitle of a book edited by Clint Willis, *The I Hate Republicans Reader: Why the GOP Is Totally Wrong About Everything* (Thunder's Mouth Press, 2003).

and swayed by mass-media political propaganda. And in a media-saturated society in which most people have short political attention spans, the easiest way to catch and hold the attention of both partisans and persuadables is to be shrill. Don't make your points in a lengthy or nuanced or gentlemanly way. Don't say that your political rivals, although intelligent persons of goodwill, are unfortunately mistaken on this or that complex matter. Instead say that they're wrong in virtually everything they do or say; charge that a third of them are wrong because they're stupid, another third because they're wicked, and the final third because they're *both* stupid and wicked.

The most conspicuous examples of this shrillness can be found on talk radio — for example, Rush Limbaugh (moderately shrill) and Michael Savage (extremely shrill) on the conservative side; and on the liberal side, the "Air America" people: Al Franken (moderate) and Randy Rhodes (extreme). In late 2005 and early 2006 the best examples of political shrillness came from ideological interest groups (see the websites of People for the American Way, the National Abortion and Reproductive Rights Action League, and Alliance for Justice, to name a few) who opposed the nomination of Samuel Alito to the United States Supreme Court. These examples happen to be from the liberal end of the ideological spectrum, but liberals have no monopoly on shrillness. Americans who see how ideological, how Manichean, and how shrill their national politics has become — a national politics largely cut off from any organic connection with local politics — might well tremble for the future of their democracy.

Republicans are more prone to accuse Democrats of being wicked than of being stupid — a reflection perhaps of the strong religious element in the Republican Party, religious people being quite naturally preoccupied with questions of virtue and wickedness.

Democrats, by contrast, are more inclined to accuse Republicans of being stupid — a reflection of the fact that liberal Democrats usually consider themselves to be intellectually superior people. Thus, Republicans were constantly talking about how immoral Bill Clinton was, while they never accused him of being stupid, and Democrats are endlessly talking about how stupid George W. Bush is. They also, it's true, accuse him of being immoral (e.g., for "lying" to the American people about the weapons of mass destruction in Iraq), but they think his stupidity is a far more salient personal attribute than his wickedness.

Adding to this shrillness is the constant need for both parties, along with their political allies (for the Democrats, such groups as the ACLU, NOW, and Planned Parenthood), to raise money from tens of thousands of relatively small contributors, the kind of people who might contribute $100 or $200 a pop. To pry the money loose, it helps enormously to be able to say that the money will be used not for mere political ends but to do battle against the forces of evil, forces that at the moment happen to be very powerful. These forces have insidious plans: to restore white supremacy; to send women back to the kitchen, where they will be kept barefoot and pregnant; to conquer the world to make it safe for the Halliburton Corporation. Send your hundred dollars in, and it's possible — just barely possible — that we'll be able to save the republic.[25]

So as the local machines and bosses lost all their former influence, replaced by affluent liberal intellectuals, the Democratic Party retained its old name but became something very different

[25] Republicans and their allies, of course, mail comparable fundraising scare letters.

from what it was in the days of my youth. You might almost say that it became a different *kind* of party, so great was the change. For one thing, this traditionally pragmatic party became an *ideological* party. (There had been some intellectual ideologues affiliated with the party in FDR's day, but their power had been very limited; the real power was held by men who were not the least bit ideological.) For another, it became unfriendly toward traditional Christianity, whereas earlier it was the party that old-fashioned Christians, both Protestants and Catholics, felt most at home in. Further, its center of gravity shifted decidedly upward on the socioeconomic scale: once a party dominated by blue-collar labor unions, now it was directed from the upper and upper-middle classes.

Again, the party became more of a nationalized/centralized party and less of a federation of local parties. Local parties now count for little; the party with headquarters in Washington counts for everything. Finally, although the spirit of partisanship has intensified, party loyalty has declined. The loyalty of the fierce ideologues is contingent: they will be loyal to the party only as long as the party adheres strictly to their ideological line. The loyalty of the non-ideological rank and file has diminished, since it no longer feels much attachment to the moribund local parties.

When all of these changes had come to pass, the nature of the new Democratic Party was fully formed. With the completion of its second great transformation, in which secularist and moral liberal ideologues first joined labor and civil-rights groups in a tripartite coalition, then rose past them to a position of dominance, the Democratic Party became the thing it is today, the thing I slowly came to recognize in my last years as a politician; the thing that today I can no longer love. It became an anti-Christian party.

Chapter 3

America's Anti-Christian Party

When I say that this great transformation of the Democratic Party turned it into an "anti-Christian party," I mean that as a kind of shorthand that sums up five essential points:

1. In the United States today, there's a Culture War between secularists and traditional Christians.
2. In this Culture War, the national Democratic Party has teamed up with the secularists and their allies.
3. The Democratic Party, once strongly identified with the common man, is now dominated by upper- and upper-middle-class ideologues.
4. Because of these changes, the Democratic Party has slipped to number-two status and will remain there until it rejects or rebuffs the secularist agenda.
5. Until the party does this, it makes little or no sense for Catholics and other traditional Christians to support the Democratic Party.

These five conclusions are the product of my observations of over forty years of social and political change, and constitute the heart of my contention about today's Democratic Party. In this chapter I will elaborate on each of them.

1. There's a Culture War taking place in the United States today, the two contending parties being secularists plus their fellow travelers on the one side, and traditional religious folk (mostly Christians) on the other.

The main division in the Culture War is a religious one; the conflict between religion and anti-religion lies at the bottom of it. With few exceptions, those on the moral conservative side — the people opposed to abortion, same-sex marriage, assisted suicide, and so forth — take religion very seriously; moreover the religion they take seriously is traditional, "old-time" religion. They're conservative Protestants and committed Catholics (along with many Eastern Orthodox Christians and Orthodox Jews) who profess belief in religious systems with high doctrinal content and strict moral rules. Conversely, their foes on the liberal side tend to be either outright secularists or believers in liberal religion — liberal religion, as I'll more fully define the term later, being an attempt to discover or create a religion that's a *via media* between secularism and traditional religion.

Here, then, is the fundamental issue at stake in the Culture War: whether old-fashioned religion, especially the old-fashioned Christianity of which traditional Catholicism is the exemplar,[26]

[26] In this book I often speak of "traditional" or "old-fashioned" or "classical" or "orthodox" Christianity, using all of these terms in a more or less synonymous way. When I simply say *Christianity* without a qualifying adjective, I usually mean traditional or old-fashioned Christianity.

will continue to play an important role in American society, such as it has for nearly four hundred years, since the first settlement of British America. Secularists are bound and determined that it will not play this role. They don't mind if traditional religious believers continue to practice their religion and religious ethic as private preferences, just as they don't mind if some people wish to collect stamps or baseball memorabilia; after all, secularists are nothing if not tolerant of individual foibles. But they want religious norms and values out of the public realm: out of government, out of law, certainly out of public schools, and generally out of the public eye as much as possible.

There are, of course, those who deny that the nation is experiencing a Culture War. Take the prominent sociologist Alan Wolfe, for example. In his *One Nation, After All* (Penguin Books, 1999) — a book with a spectacularly long subtitle: *What Middle-Class Americans Really Think About God, Country, Family, Racism, Welfare, Immigration, Homosexuality, Work, the Right, the Left, and Each Other* — he shows that Americans agree on almost all major values. If there's so much agreement, he concludes, how can there be a Culture War? He grants that there might be a kind of culture war going on among intellectuals of the political Right and political Left;

This is because I hold that "modern" or "liberal" Christianity is Christianity only in an equivocal or Pickwickian sense of the word. I say this, no doubt, because of my Catholic views as to what counts as genuine Christianity; but I also say it because of my study of history. The thing called "modern" or "liberal" Christianity is a relatively recent phenomenon, a byproduct of the eighteenth-century Enlightenment; it isn't Christianity as it emerged during the first few centuries of the Roman Empire and as it was understood by almost all Christians for the next 1,800 years.

battles like that are the kind of thing intellectuals enjoy. But his research has convinced him that among ordinary non-intellectual Americans there's no such war; instead there's a great cultural consensus.

Now, if Wolfe had done his research during the 1850s, he could have shown that Americans, both North and South, agreed on almost all values — indeed, likely more than they do today — and so, he might have concluded cheerfully, it would have been absurd to predict a coming civil war. This is because Wolfe neglects to note that major cultural divisions don't depend on the *quantity* of the disagreements so much as on their *quality*. Qualitatively speaking, there was one big cultural disagreement between North and South: it had to do with slavery, the South's "peculiar institution," and this single disagreement was enough to tear the nation apart.

Today Americans differ on but a small number of value questions: abortion, homosexuality, euthanasia, pornography, prayer in schools, and a few others. But although they're few, so important to both sides are these issues that they have similarly been able to rend our society — if not quite to the point of bloodshed.

Wolfe isn't the only person to deny the existence of a Culture War. Most political liberals, with rare exceptions, also deny it. These deniers usually suggest that the myth of the Culture War was invented, or at least given widespread currency, by Pat Buchanan in his notorious speech at the 1992 Republican National Convention; and that the myth has been kept alive since then by Republicans for crass political and fundraising purposes. From the liberal Democratic point of view, this deceitful strategy has worked. They believe that vast numbers of working- and lower-middle-class Americans have been so hoodwinked by conservative propaganda that they've allowed their economic interests, the natural protector of which is the Democratic Party, to be overruled by their moral-religious fears; and the result is that the Republican Party has come to power in Washington. This Republican takeover of Washington has given some symbolic satisfaction to social-conservative voters, but it has given most of these voters little or nothing in the way of economic satisfaction while conferring immense financial benefits on the people who really run the Republican Party: big businesses and the rich. So runs the liberal-Democratic analysis of what they are pleased to call the "myth" of the Culture War.

There's some truth to this analysis — some, but not much. It's true that big business remains what it has almost always been: the dominant force in the Republican Party.[27] It's even true that to date the Republicans in Washington have given moral-religious conservatives little more than symbolic victories in Culture War battles (although these victories might eventually become more substantial now that President Bush has placed two apparently conservative justices on the Supreme Court). And it's without question true that Republican politicians and conservative fund-raisers have been able to harness culture-war anxieties to reap many votes and a great deal of money.

But think of the adage: "Just because you're paranoid, it doesn't mean they're not out to get you." Just because Republicans and conservatives are making political hay out of the alleged threat Democrats and liberals pose to Christian values, it doesn't follow that the threat doesn't exist. Many liberals believe that moral-religious

[27] I've noticed over the years that my Republican friends get upset whenever I suggest that theirs is the party of the rich. However, I don't propose to prove this proposition here. If Republican readers are offended by my contention, I won't object if they chalk it up to the anti-Republican prejudices I acquired during my long lifetime as a Democrat.

conservatives are mostly boobs and nincompoops, and thus easily fooled; it's no wonder to them that unscrupulous Republican leaders can succeed in tricking them into having intellectual hallucinations — for instance, that liberals are the enemies of Christianity. But most moral-religious conservatives are *not* boobs or nincompoops; if they believe that their values and their religion are under attack from liberals, they're very probably not hallucinating. Democrats would do well not to dismiss their fears so easily.

In logic textbooks there's a valid argument form called *modus tollens*. It goes like this:

> If p, then q.
> But not q.
> Therefore not p.

To illustrate:

> If your aunt is the queen of England, she lives in Buckingham Palace.
> But your aunt does not live in Buckingham Palace.
> Therefore your aunt is not the queen of England.

Or to come to the point at hand:

> If Christianity is the true religion of God, then abortion, homosexual conduct, suicide, and so forth are morally wrong.
> But abortion, homosexual conduct, suicide, and so forth are *not* morally wrong.
> Therefore Christianity is not the true religion of God.

Traditional Christians of all kinds (including Catholics) assert the first proposition. Secularists and their allies assert the second, and by asserting it, they're also asserting, at least by implication, proposition three.

To understand what's at stake here, it's crucial to recognize that certain Christian beliefs are *essential:* elements that Christianity can't lose without ceasing to be itself. Remove one or more of these elements, and you no longer have traditional Christianity, whether Protestant or Catholic; the traditional Christian thing is destroyed, and it becomes another thing. Most of these beliefs are theological — that God exists, that God is a Trinity, that Jesus Christ is both true God and true man, and so forth. But no less essential are certain moral beliefs — that non-marital sex is wrong, for instance, and so are unmarried cohabitation, homosexual conduct, abortion, suicide, and euthanasia. Thus, when moral liberals defend such practices, they're denying the legitimacy of traditional Christianity no less than if they had attacked the doctrine of Christ's divinity. In either case, they're waging metaphorical war against the old-time Christian religion.

If it's obvious to conservative Christians that their religion is under attack from liberals, and if this should be obvious to any impartial and objective observer, why is it far from obvious to most liberals themselves? Why do they deny it? There are four answers to this question.

First, there are some moral liberals (a small minority) who hate Christianity and are deliberately out to destroy it, but they've decided that a "stealth" campaign against the religion would have a much better chance of success than an open campaign. And so, when speaking in public (and usually when speaking in private as well), they stress the positive aspects of their program, not the negative. That is, they tell you what values they favor without reminding you of the Christian values they oppose. They say, for instance, that they favor sexual freedom, not that they oppose the Christian value of chastity; or that they favor a woman's right to choose, not that they oppose the Christian notion that human life has absolute value from the moment of conception; or that they favor equal treatment for gays and lesbians, not that they oppose the Christian idea that some sexual relationships are natural and some unnatural; and so on. Above all, they carefully abstain from telling you that they're out to destroy Christianity; indeed, they profess to be great believers in religious freedom.

Second, the great majority of moral liberals are not *consciously* aiming at Christianity's destruction or even at the defeat of Christian values and Christian morality. What they *do* want is a society made safe for sexual freedom, abortion, same-sex marriage, physician-assisted suicide, and so forth; how this might affect Christianity isn't their concern. If Christianity in America continues to flourish, that's okay with them, as long as sexual freedom, abortion, gay marriage, and euthanasia are also allowed to flourish. It hasn't occurred to them — or, if it has occurred, it hasn't sunk in — that Christianity will not be able to flourish simultaneously with their own values; if one prevails, the other will be defeated.

A third reason is that secularists and moral liberals generally have little understanding of Christianity. At first this seems odd, since they live in a society that has had a Christian tone to it from its very beginning. How could any educated American be ignorant of Christianity? But religious ignorance among Americans — or rather, the ignorance of religions other than one's own — isn't confined to secularists; it's pervasive among religious folk as well. Traditional religions tend to teach children the particulars of their own religion and little about others, while liberal religions stress ecumenical tolerance and the similarities among faiths, ignoring dogmatic distinctions and discouraging curiosity about other belief systems. As a result, these days Catholics don't know much about Protestantism, and Protestants don't know much about Catholicism, and Jews don't know much about either. American Christians have scant knowledge of Islam, Buddhism, and Hinduism, and they don't do much better in their knowledge of the varieties of Judaism. In such a cultural environment, it's unsurprising that secularists and moral liberals too should be ignorant of the content of traditional Christianity. And if they're ignorant, it should likewise be unsurprising that they don't see how their championship of sexual freedom, abortion, same-sex marriage, and so forth is tantamount to an assault on traditional Christianity.

Finally, while liberals don't believe that they're attacking Christianity, they *do* believe that Christianity is attacking liberalism. Yet they don't construe this attack as part of a culture war, for a war, like a tango, takes two, and secularists don't believe they're fighting a war. Secularists and moral liberals view Christian belligerence rather as a kind of imperialism. They see an effort by old-fashioned and narrow-minded Christians to capture control of government and establish a "theocracy" by which they can impose their beliefs and values on the rest of American society. This, of course, is nothing less than an attempt to undermine the Constitution; thus, when liberals resist this theocratic crusade, they see themselves not as making war on Christianity, but simply as defending democracy and the American way of life.

In a certain sense, of course, there have been cultural conflicts between Christians and anti-Christians since the earliest days of

Christianity. Indeed, as I will show later, there has been some kind of culture war going on in the United States since the founding of the republic. But the present-day Culture War (the one with initial capital letters) dates back only to the cultural revolution that began in the 1960s. This spectacular upsurge of secularist, anti-Christianity impulses was marked by a generalized rebellion against authority: the authority of government, educators, religion, family — and above all the authority of tradition. Among the notable outcomes of this rebellion were the so-called "sexual revolution" and a turn toward pacifism.

Such outcomes had political implications. Secularists soon began promoting a political agenda that was favorable toward sexual freedom (especially the right to abortion) and unfavorable toward military action. Conversely, traditional Christians, perceiving secularists as the enemies of their religion, soon began promoting a contrary political agenda. These two cultural parties eventually formed alliances with the nation's two dominant political parties — cultural liberals or secularists with the Democrats, cultural conservatives or traditional Christians with the Republicans — and today play major roles in them.

As a result of the Culture War, American politics has become something like the politics of France during the Third Republic. The French nation was politically divided between Catholics, who held that the "true France" was the France of Catholicism and Joan of Arc and the long line of Capetian kings, and anticlericals, who held that the true France was the France of Voltaire, Rousseau, and the Revolution. Third Republic politics was a protracted struggle between those who hated the Catholic Church and those who loved it. Similarly, American politics today has increasingly become a struggle between those who hate traditional Christianity and those who love it. Republicans by and large profess to be the friends of those who love traditional Christianity, while Democrats have even more thoroughly offered themselves as the friends of those who hate it.

> *2. In this Culture War, the national Democratic Party has teamed up with the secularists and their allies; in so doing, it has become a de facto anti-Christian party.*

If the Democratic Party has come to be dominated by anti-Christian secularists and their allies, the Democratic Party can rightly be called an anti-Christian party.

Now, when I say that the Democratic Party has become an anti-Christian party, I don't mean that it's anti-Christian in the way that right-wing political parties have often been anti-Semitic, or in the way that the Democratic Party of the post–Civil War South was anti-Negro. The aim of the Democrats is not to treat Christians as second-class citizens;[28] their objection is not to Christians as individuals but to their belief system. I say they're "anti-Christian," but this is shorthand for saying they're anti-Christianity.

And when I say the "aim" of the party is anti-Christian, I don't mean that this is a conscious or deliberate aim, at least not for the great majority of Democrats. Their anti-Christianity "aim" is no more than a de facto aim. The *effect* of their political efforts is anti-Christian, even if this isn't what they consciously intend. Or to put this another way: they're *objectively* anti-Christian, even if they're not *subjectively* so. And so I don't contend that Catholic

[28] Secularists, most of whom are Democrats, do perhaps discriminate against Christians in the hiring and promotion practices of leading universities; but this is an exception to the rule.

politicians who toe the party line on abortion or homosexuality are insincere or hypocritical in their religious professions. Not at all. I have no reason to believe that they're anything other than sincere believers.

I must also emphasize that when I say the Democratic Party has become an anti-Christian party, I haven't forgotten that there are other elements in the party with no interest in the destruction of Christianity: neither organized labor nor organized blacks believe it's in the interest of their constituents to promote abortion, homosexuality, same-sex marriage, or assisted suicide. However, in the coalition that makes up the national Democratic Party, and on the principle that politics makes for strange bedfellows, both the labor and civil-rights sections of the party have fallen in line, at least nominally, with the social agenda of the increasingly dominant secularist/moral liberal section; they might not be enthusiastic about this agenda, but they do little or nothing to oppose it, and they usually support it when it comes to decision-making time.

Analogously, when someone says that the Republican Party is dominated by big business and the wealthy, he doesn't mean that only rich people belong to it. Since the numbers of the wealthy are comparatively few, if such a party expects to win elections in a democratic political system, it will need many non-rich supporters; and so the Republican Party has always had. Thus, to say that the Republican Party is dominated by the rich is not to deny that most Republican voters, in fact, are not rich; and likewise, to say that the Democratic Party is dominated by secularists and anti-Christians is not to deny that most Democratic voters are not anti-Christian secularists.

3. *The Democratic Party, once strongly identified with the working classes and the common man, is no longer a small-d*

democratic party; it's now a party largely dominated by upper- and upper-middle-class ideologues.

An ideology isn't something that falls from the sky. It isn't a disembodied abstraction that haunts the atmosphere. No, it's a system of beliefs and values held by an identifiable group of people, usually by a certain social class or ethnic/racial group. Members of the group hold that philosophy because they believe it to be true, of course, but they normally believe it to be true because it coincides with, and promotes, what they feel to be their vital interests.

Groups who hold an ideology use it to serve three purposes. First, it's used to justify the group itself. Second, it's used as a weapon with which to attack, and to defend against, the group's enemies. Third, it's used to persuade those who, at the moment, are neutrals, neither friends nor enemies of the group.

Secularism, including its ethic of moral liberalism, is such an ideology. It's a belief system typically held by upper-middle-class Americans. This isn't to say that everybody from the upper-middle classes holds this philosophy, but it is disproportionately held — *very* disproportionately so — by persons of that socioeconomic status and by persons who have realistic aspirations to that status. Nor is it to say that nobody else holds the ideology: there are those from other classes who are convinced of its truth; and there are those who hold it because they feel a strong dislike for Christians. Yet the principal bearer of the secularist ideology is the upper-middle class.[29]

[29] It's an interesting fact that in the 2004 presidential campaign, the Democratic candidate was able to raise more money than the Republican incumbent.

These people use their ideology to justify themselves in their own eyes. ("We hold a true philosophy of life; thus, we're morally and intellectually superior people; and therefore we and our children are entitled to the many social and economic privileges we actually possess.") They use it as a weapon against their enemies, who are mainly Christians of working-class and lower-middle-class status.[30] ("These old-school Christians are ignorant, and in their ignorance they're dangerous to the well-being of American democracy, not to mention the international community. Therefore, they must be defeated — or at least their false beliefs must be defeated, thereby liberating these unfortunates to see the truth.") And the ideology is used to persuade neutrals. ("Do you want America turned into a theocracy? Do you want the government in your bedroom? Do you want your gay cousin to be unable to live a life of married fidelity and contentment?")

The counter-ideology faced by secularism is traditional Christianity, whose principal (although again, by no means exclusive) bearers are people from the working and lower-middle classes.[31] Whatever other functions Christianity might have (e.g., saving souls), it also has the threefold social function typical of ideologies: self-justification, attack on enemies, and persuasion of neutrals.

[30] American society may be thought of as divided into five social classes or socioeconomic groups: upper, upper-middle, lower-middle, working, and impoverished. I refer to the upper and upper-middle classes as the "higher" classes, the lower-middle and working as the "middling" classes, and the impoverished as the "lower" class.

[31] Some readers will object that Christianity isn't an ideology (as above defined); rather, it's a revelation from God. This is a theologically valid point, but for purposes of the present discussion it's enough that Christianity functions socially and psychologically very like an ideology.

Why is secularism so popular among the higher classes? Consider a number of reasons. First, to justify their many social privileges, the higher classes want to hold a philosophy that's different from and superior to the philosophy held by their social inferiors. If their inferiors tend to be Christian, the higher classes will then have to be non- or anti-Christian. (The reverse of this took place in France during the Third Republic. Since proletarians tended to be atheistic, the bourgeoisie had to be Catholic.) Second, the higher classes are better educated than the middling classes; not only have they had more years of schooling, but they've attended colleges and universities of the highest prestige. Now, empiricist assumptions have increasingly come to underlay all modern — and postmodern — education, and so these first-class institutions have taken for granted a nonreligious interpretation of reality. Third, the great social, economic, and political power possessed by people in the higher classes makes it difficult for them, at least while they're in the prime of life, to feel what serious religious believers constantly feel — namely, that our poor human power is as nothing compared with the omnipotent providence of God. Finally, people with money live in a world that provides them with an immense menu of choices: choices in clothing, jobs, places to live, restaurants to eat at, wines to drink, destinations to travel to, theaters and concerts to attend, books to read, and so on. How natural, then, it seems to them that people should have choices and options when it comes to such matters as abortion and sexual partners; how strange it would be if there were no choices in these matters.

Conversely, what is it that causes traditional Christianity to be so popular an ideology among the middling classes? First, it enables them to defend themselves against the disdain and contempt felt for them by the higher classes. "You privileged people might have the money and power," they say, "but we're closer to God; and it's better to be close to God than to be rich." Second, Christianity imposes a moral discipline on them that they can't afford to be without. If you have lots of money, you have a greater margin of safety in your life; even if you do something reckless, you can have a safe landing. But those in the middling classes have little margin of safety; they need strict religion to preserve them and their children from moral or prudential blunders. Finally, people whose power, choices, and possessions are very limited have less difficulty believing in the providential power of God and less difficulty in accepting moral and intellectual boundaries. The rich and powerful are more apt to put faith in their own agency and possessions.

Further, the attraction of Christianity, while stronger among the middling than the higher classes, is strongest of all among those in the middle who are married and have children. There's something about raising children that makes persons more morally serious than they used to be. They take longer views, and they become more sensitive to the dangers lurking in the world — not just the physical dangers but the moral dangers as well. They become less tolerant of persons who are reckless in their behavior (even if they themselves were equally reckless in their younger days), whether those persons live next door or halfway around the world. A God whose job it is to superintend both the biggest things and the smallest things seems to them a plausible God.

Curiously, when speaking of secularism, moral-religious conservatives rarely resort to class analysis. Occasionally they'll suggest that secularists are "elitists," but this is more name-calling than it is analysis. The reason for this reluctance, I suggest, is that class analysis in politics has always been pretty much a monopoly of the political Left, most notably the Marxian Left, but also the liberal Left. It has been used to argue that the great wealth, power, and privilege of the well-to-do are illegitimate. Not surprisingly, then, moral conservatives who are well-to-do don't approve of this kind of analysis, even when it's used, as I've just used it, to erode the legitimacy of secularist ideologues. For if it can be used against affluent secularists today, it can be used against even more affluent non-secularists tomorrow. Since today's Republican coalition involves an alliance between Wall Street and Main Street — between big-business interests and traditional Christian believers — and since Wall Street is still the dominant power in the party, it follows that the use of social-class analysis by moral-religious conservatives is taboo. Main Street understands that Wall Street would be offended by such analysis, and Main Street also understands that it will be able to accomplish little or nothing within the Republican Party without the cooperation, or at least the permission, of Wall Street.

When the day arrives that moral-religious conservatives feel free to use social-class analysis in their struggle against secularism, you'll know that the day has also arrived when big-money interests no longer rule the roost in the Republican Party. When that day arrives — if it ever does — the Republican Party will have ceased to be a party of the rich; it will have become a plebeian party.

4. As a consequence of having alienated non-affluent Christian voters, the Democratic Party has lost its position as America's number-one political party. It will remain number two until it expels or at least marginalizes the anti-Christians currently wielding great influence in its ranks.

As the Democratic Party's affiliation with anti-Christian secularism becomes stronger and more evident, more and more conservative Protestants and orthodox Catholics are defecting from the party of their parents and grandparents. Who can be surprised at that? It makes no sense for Christian voters to give their time, money, and votes to a party that has become the tool of forces waging cultural war against their religion. Increasingly these Christian, culturally conservative voters are turning to the Republican Party, which in the Culture War has proved friendlier to Christianity.

But what, it might be objected, of the millions of Christians who continue to support the Democratic Party and its candidates? I think we're witnessing a kind of "culture lag" at work. Many Christian voters have recognized the new secularist character of the Democratic Party, but a great many haven't. There are two major groups that haven't yet come to recognize the transformation that has taken place in the party since the days of John Kennedy and Lyndon Johnson. One is older voters who came of age during the time of Kennedy and Johnson, or even some of the very old ones who remember FDR and Truman. The other group is African-American voters. Once upon a time, between the death of Abraham Lincoln and the first election of Franklin Roosevelt, for a black to be a Democrat was almost unthinkable. The Democratic Party of the South was the party of white supremacy, while the party outside the South, although only moderately racist itself, had no strong objection to the racism of its Southern co-partisans. But since the presidency of Lyndon Johnson and his Civil Rights Act (1964) and Voting Rights Act (1965), exactly the opposite has been true: to be black has been to be Democrat; to be a black Republican has been virtually unthinkable.

Both these groups — older voters and black voters — have a kind of "essentialist" understanding of the Democratic Party;

which is to say, they think the party has a kind of timeless and unchanging "essence" and is therefore the same party today as it was in the days when they first fell in love with it. If I'm right in saying this, then the condition of the Democratic Party is likely to become even worse in the future than it is today. For one thing, older voters will gradually die off; for another, the essentialist understanding of the party can't persist indefinitely in the face of contrary evidence. In time, older voters and African-American voters — both of whom tend to be culturally conservative — will gradually wake up to the new reality of the Democratic Party, and many of them won't like what they see.[32]

If the United States were a predominantly secularist or near-secularist nation, an anti-Christian strategy would be politically expedient; just as in Germany in the post–World War I era, an anti-Semitic strategy was politically expedient, and just as in the American South for nearly a century after the Civil War, an anti-Negro strategy was politically expedient. But although secularism is stronger now than it has ever been, the United States is still predominantly religious, indeed predominantly Christian. This isn't to say that these Christians are all of the traditional type, for many Catholics and Protestants have drifted away from orthodoxy intellectually and even morally. Nonetheless their "hearts" remain

[32] Lest my comments on the "essentialism" of older voters and black voters seem condescending, I'll point out that I am myself an older voter and that I too have something of an essentialist view of the party. I realize that the party has changed, changed almost utterly, over the last thirty or forty years, but I cling to the belief that much of its old goodness remains at its well-hidden inner core, and I cling to the hope that this old goodness will someday re-emerge — if only we can get rid of the alien encrustations that have concealed the core.

attached by many strings to the old-time religion, and if it comes to a battle between secularism and Christianity, the sympathies of most of them will be with the latter. Being the anti-Christian party is political suicide for Democrats, as election returns increasingly show.

If the Democratic Party wishes to hold on to voters who are thinking of jumping ship, and if it wishes to win back voters who jumped ship some years ago, it will have to persuade its affluent secularist members either to cease pushing their agenda or else to take their agenda and leave the party. For the Democratic Party and its national electoral prospects, the best thing would be for these people to join the Green Party or to create some new ultra-left party, returning control of the Democratic Party to organized labor and minorities. But this is unlikely; secularists and their supporters are now too powerful to be purged from the party.

The second-best thing would be for affluent secularists to remain in the party while abandoning the more "offensive" parts of their agenda. But this too is unlikely to happen. What's the point of gaining control of a major political party, secularists would rightly ask, if you can't then use that control to promote your agenda?

The third-best thing would be for affluent secularists and their friends to disguise themselves, to pretend that they're not what they really are. The secularist element in the party can license Democratic politicians to speak of "faith" in their personal lives, of their belief in "values," of how they'd like to lower the rate of abortion in America, of the importance of strong families, and so on. Such rhetoric would create the illusion that they're moral moderates, even moral conservatives, while they nonetheless continue to help enact the moral liberal agenda in undiluted form. This deceptive rhetoric is already being heard, and there's a strong likelihood that it will continue to be heard — and even to be effective, at least in the short term. But you can't fool all the people all the time, and so in the long term the party will continue to slide downhill as long as affluent secularist ideologues play a major role in shaping its conduct.

> 5. *Until the party expels or marginalizes its secularist element, it makes little or no sense for Catholics and other traditional Christians to support the Democratic Party.*

Here we see one of the main reasons Christians of the traditional kind, both Protestant and Catholic, are drifting away from the Democratic Party. "Why should I support a party that's the enemy of my religion?" they ask. Likewise, Christians who continue to support today's Democratic Party increasingly experience feelings of cognitive dissonance[33] and will discover that one way to eliminate those unpleasant dissonant feelings is by ceasing to vote for Democrats.

A case can be made, of course, that it *does* make sense for religiously *liberal* Catholics and Protestants to continue supporting the Democratic Party, despite its anti-Christian tendencies. If secularism undermines orthodox Christianity long enough and well enough, it will leave liberal denominations as the only Christian game in town. Victories of secularism over traditional orthodoxy will conduce, a Christian liberal might surmise, to the long-term triumph of Christian liberalism. This argument, I say, can be

[33] The inventor of the Cognitive Dissonance Theory was the social-psychologist Leon Festinger. For an instructive and entertaining application of the theory, see his book, *When Prophecy Fails* (University of Minnesota Press, 1956).

made — but it's a foolish argument. It reminds me of the argument made by Communists who greeted the rise of Nazism in Germany with delight: in defeating the only rival the Communists had on the left, the Social Democrats, Nazism would radicalize all leftists and drive them into the ranks of the Communist Party. The victories of Hitler, they concluded, would conduce to the long-term triumph of Communism. Of course the Communists underestimated Hitler and the Nazis while exaggerating the potential attractiveness of the Communist option; likewise liberal Christians underestimate the anti-Christian power of secularism and greatly overestimate the attractiveness of the liberal Christian option.

In truth liberal Christianity, because it essentially rejects the dogmatic principle in religion (see Appendix III), has no long-run staying power. It's more or less parasitical upon traditional Christianity. It's a halfway house between traditional Christianity and outright infidelity, where people dissatisfied with the orthodox brand of religion they were brought up in pause on their way to unbelief. Some might even pause there for a lifetime, but this stopping-place can't endure on its own. For one thing, the beliefs of a liberal church have no stability: committed to endless modernization, the church finds that the progressive doctrines of today are no longer sufficiently forward-thinking tomorrow. For another, liberalism tends not to be passed on over generations; the entire history of Christian liberalism, from its beginning in eighteenth-century Germany and England until today, testifies to this truth. If liberal Christianity is to survive, it needs orthodox Christianity to keep providing it with new recruits; were orthodoxy to collapse, the liberal collapse would soon follow.

Now, it might make good *logical* sense for Catholics to secede from the Democratic Party, but whether they will actually do so depends on a number of factors. For one, it depends on how

"Catholic" a person is. Those who are little more than nominal Catholics, practicing the religion hardly at all and identifying with it only out of habit or family tradition, aren't greatly offended by the party's alliance with the forces of secularism; for these nominal Catholics are virtually secularists themselves. Neither are liberal Catholics greatly offended, for they regard the defeat of orthodox Catholicism as a gain, a door opening to a new-and-improved brand of Catholicism. It's Catholics who practice their faith regularly, who assent strongly to the doctrines of their religion and at least try to follow them, who are most likely to conclude that supporting the Democratic Party has become logically — or even morally — untenable.

How many Catholics of this variety will there turn out to be? Much depends upon the quality of clerical leadership, especially the leadership given (or, as is too often the case, not given) by bishops. For some forty years now, this leadership has been strikingly ineffective; the most infamous example of this ineffectiveness, the recent scandal of clerical sex abuse and cover-up, is only the spectacular tip of the iceberg.

It's well to keep in mind, however, that the Catholic Church has had many declines and revivals in the course of its long history. It's always possible that a new generation of strong and effective bishops will emerge; in fact, there are some signs that such a new generation is emerging at this very moment. If the leaders of the Democratic Party are in the habit of praying for election victories, they should ask the Lord that he not inspire such a religious revival in the American Catholic Church. For if he does, Catholic men and women in the pews will become more orthodox in their opinions and attitudes; they'll find the Democratic Party more and more unappetizing; and the numbers of the party's scorned lovers will continue to grow.

Nonetheless, for the present there are many Catholics who happily remain Democrats — both among the party's rank and file and in positions of party leadership. Some don't fully comprehend the implications of secularist dominance of the party, while others believe that secularists and Christians aren't mortally opposed but can work together in a mutually beneficial partnership. If this were true, a Catholic could indeed remain a Democrat without logical or moral contradiction. But I contend that there's a great abyss between traditional Christianity and secularism (and secularism's partner, liberal Christianity) — a vast, radical divide that makes such cooperation impossible. In the second part of the book, we'll look more closely at this divide and what it means.

Part II

The Party and the Church Are Irreconcilable

Chapter 4

The Catholic-Secularist Abyss

"It is come, I know not how, to be taken for granted by many persons that Christianity is not so much as a subject of inquiry; but that it is now, at length, discovered to be fictitious. And accordingly they treat it as if, in the present age, this were an agreed point among all people of discernment; and nothing remained but to set it up as a principal subject of mirth and ridicule, as it were by way of reprisals for its having so long interrupted the pleasures of the world."

Joseph Butler, *The Analogy of Religion* (1736)

So it's manifest that the modern, secularist Democratic Party has embraced moral liberal principles — notably abortion, sexual liberation, and, increasingly, euthanasia — that directly counter those commonly known to be held by traditional Christianity. I've argued that these principles can prevail in American culture only at the expense of Christianity; thus, a Catholic, or any traditional Christian, who doesn't want his religion diminished should cease supporting the party until it renounces or moderates its affiliation with secularism.

Some might object that I protest too much. Surely on balance there's more for a Catholic to like than to dislike within the Democratic Party. And if secularists have made incursions into the party's power structure, well, that's unfortunate, but politics is always about compromise. So why can't Catholics and secularists, despite their very obvious and in some ways very important differences, reach a working truce and continue to work together within the same party? Why can't they both find a place under a big Democratic tent?

After all, can their differences be any greater than those which once existed between Southern white Protestants and Northern Catholics, most of these Catholics being immigrants or the children and grandchildren of immigrants? Neither group very much liked the other; in fact, they had rather a lively distaste for one another.

Yet from the end of the Civil War until the 1960s — a period of one hundred years — these were the twin pillars of the national Democratic Party. Both groups understood that they had to stick together to promote their separate interests. Their alliance splendidly illustrated the proverb about politics making for strange bedfellows.

Would an alliance between Catholics and secularists be any stranger than this old alliance? Secularists are hardly any more hostile toward the Catholic religion than Southern white Protestants were during the century following the Civil War. Granted, many secularists probably believe that the world would be a better place if Catholicism were to vanish from it. But didn't the old-fashioned Protestants believe the same — and with more vigor and venom? After all, among the core beliefs of the "old-time religion" was (and for some of its adherents, still is) that Catholicism is a false and perverted version of Christianity; a paganized syncretism; the "Whore of Babylon" prophesied in the book of Revelation. If Catholics for a century could sleep in the same political bed with Protestants of this stripe, why can't they today sleep with secularists?

The answer is simple: Southern white Protestants didn't like the Catholic religion, to be sure, and in their sermons and Sunday Schools they relentlessly found fault with it. But they didn't use the Democratic Party to promote their anti-Catholicism. By contrast, secularists *are* using their position of dominance in the Democratic Party effectively to destroy Catholicism in America (and old-fashioned Protestantism too). Through the party, they're vigorously promoting moral values that clash so directly with those of traditional Christianity that if they're validated in American culture, traditional Christianity must be invalidated.

There has long been a serious gap between the religion of Catholics and the religion of conservative Protestants. There's divergence on certain points of doctrine, authority, and worship. There are old grudges and prejudices. But the gap isn't nearly so great as to preclude cooperation, for in fact they still agree on most articles of faith and moral beliefs. Between Catholicism and secularism, however, the gap of beliefs — of philosophies or worldviews — is so deep that it may be called an abyss.

The nineteenth-century French philosopher-sociologist August Comte said, "Ideas govern the world." It follows from this that people who differ radically in their ideas will find it difficult to cooperate on matters of importance. Catholics and secularists hold radically different principles about the limits of knowledge and the nature of reality, and from these differences flow conflicting — in fact, irreconcilable — theories of morality.

Empiricism versus revelation

Let's look, first of all, at their contrasting theories of knowledge. With almost no exceptions, secularists are empiricists; that is to say, they hold that it's impossible to have any knowledge that doesn't come to us through the senses. "Unless I can see it or hear it or touch it or taste it or smell it, I can't believe it": this is the attitude of the typical secularist.[34] An empiricist won't believe that there can be any such thing as knowledge of immaterial entities — God, for example, or immortal souls. Being by definition immaterial, these are not the kind of things that could be observed, even if we had finer and more powerful senses. Nor will he believe that moral good and evil, or rightness and wrongness, are objective qualities; how could they be, if they exhibit no sense qualities? What color is goodness? How long is it? How much does it weigh?

[34] Of course, they don't mean that all objects of knowledge must be directly observable by the unaided senses; it's okay to use instruments such as microscopes or telescopes. Nor do they mean that all objects of knowledge must be observable at all. Some objects are so small (e.g., electrons) or so remote in space (black holes) or in time (the Big Bang) that their existence can only be inferred. But these inferences rest on data obtained by the senses, and the objects of these inferences have sense characteristics that could be directly observed if our senses were finer and more powerful. For a philosophical expression of a view almost identical with this, see A. J. Ayer's *Language, Truth, and Logic* (1936), especially chapter 1, "The Elimination of Metaphysics," where the famous "verification principle" is explained. Ayer's book was intended to introduce the English-speaking world to the philosophy of the Logical Positivists (or Vienna Circle), a school of thought that flourished in the years between the two world wars.

Catholicism, by contrast, holds that the human mind is capable of obtaining knowledge of God — not complete or comprehensive knowledge, to be sure, but at least partial knowledge. It teaches that the existence of God can be proven by human reason; more important, it teaches that God has revealed to humankind, through the Church and the Bible, knowledge about himself. This divine revelation, moreover, contains instruction about many other matters than can't be known on an empiricist basis: knowledge about the nature (or rather, natures) of Jesus Christ, about life after death, about the conditions of salvation, about questions of morality, and so forth.

Further, Catholicism has always held that there's a "natural" or non-revealed knowledge of moral principles possessed by all humans. This is the moral knowledge referred to by St. Paul in his letter to the Romans (2:15), where he says of the Gentiles that they have "a law written in their hearts." Knowledge of this "natural law" is not, to be sure, as complete a knowledge of morality as is given by divine revelation, but it will serve for most earthly purposes, and indeed has served for the great majority — the non-Christian and non-Jewish majority — of the human race. We apprehend this knowledge not through the senses but by the operation of what philosophers call "moral intuition," more commonly known as the "conscience."

Naturalism versus supernaturalism

Secularists are in almost all cases *naturalists;* that is to say, they believe that nature is all there is, that there's no realm of being that transcends nature — and hence, no God and no community of immortal souls. Catholics, by contrast, believe that there is a supernatural realm — that is, an afterlife. In its best section (heaven) are to be found God and his saints, in its worst section (hell) dwell fallen angels and great human sinners, and in its middle section (purgatory) live sinners who are undergoing a process of purification to prepare them for heaven. Moreover, Catholics believe that this super- or trans-natural realm is far more important than the natural world in which we live at the moment. We live *here* but a brief moment — eighty or ninety years at most. We'll live *there* forever. Catholics further believe that there can be a two-way communication between the two realms. God and the saints hear our prayers, and we receive God's graces.

I should add that when I say that "Catholics" believe in this Dante-like view of the supernatural universe, I don't mean that a Gallup Poll would discover that these are the actual beliefs of all, or even most, American Catholics. Many Catholics, like their Protestant fellow-Americans, have discarded the ancient Christian belief in purgatory, while others refuse to believe that a loving God could condemn any of his children to everlasting punishment in hell.

And I certainly don't mean that the average Catholic focuses more of his daily concerns on the supernatural realm than on the natural. He likely spends more time worrying about his job, family life, taxes, investments, diet, and tennis game than about how he stands in relation to the world of supernatural entities. I mean, rather, that these are the official teachings of the Catholic Church, teachings therefore that genuinely orthodox Catholics adhere to — even if they don't always live in accordance with those teachings.

And so we have these two contrasts — these two immense contrasts — between the secularist worldview and the Catholic: empiricism versus revelation, naturalism versus supernaturalism. These quite naturally lead to further contrasts in matters of morality.

Moral objectivism versus subjectivism

The first of these contrasts has to do with the question of whether moral values and rules of moral duty are *objective* or *subjective*. An objective moral value isn't a manmade creation; it exists independently of human wishes, just as much as does the roundness of the earth. Of course, its existence is a very different kind of existence than that of the earth: the earth is a material thing; a moral value or rule is not. And we know that the earth is round through sense experience, whereas we know that stealing is wrong by means of moral intuition or the conscience.

When we say that moral rules or values are subjective, conversely, we mean that they're manmade creations — invented by some group (a religion, a society, a sub-society) or individual. Thus, there can be no true knowledge of (or meaningful arguments about) rightness or wrongness, goodness or badness. We can know that this or that religion or society holds adultery to be wrong or courage to be right, but we can't know whether adultery really is wrong or courage really is right. The most a moral decree can mean is this: "We disapprove of adultery and approve of courage, and we strongly demand that you do the same; and if you don't, we'll find some way of punishing you."

Catholics believe that moral values and the rules of morality are objective, not created by humans but created by God. These rules and values are either the positive commandments of God or they're inferred from human nature (and thus also created by God, since God is the author of nature). Secularists believe that moral values and rules are subjective, rooted in nothing more solid than personal or cultural preference.

I must add by way of clarification that a secularist *should* believe this, if he is to be consistent with his empiricist theory of knowledge. But not every secularist is consistent when it comes to questions of morality; in fact, very few of them are. Rather, it usually depends on his attitude toward the conduct in question. If you tell him that abortion or fornication is wrong, he'll reply that it might be wrong according your subjective judgment or opinion, but it's right according to the subjective opinion or judgment of others. But if you stomp violently on his toe or take a sledgehammer to his automobile, he'll forget his empiricism and subjectivism and say that what you've done is really and truly wrong.

The secularist, it turns out, has a considerable rhetorical advantage. On the one hand, when he wishes to dismiss *your* views, he can adhere closely to subjectivism and tell you that your moral judgments are no more than an expression of the subjective preferences of you or your group. On the other, if he wishes to give vent to a temper of moral indignation, he can temporarily lay aside his subjectivist theory and denounce you for your genuine wickedness.

Absolutism versus relativism

Catholics will allow that certain rules of morality admit of exceptions or careful distinctions. For instance, it's wrong to tell a lie, but there are some circumstances — rare no doubt — in which it's morally permissible, even perhaps morally obligatory, to stretch the truth. We're duty-bound to obey the laws laid down by legitimate civil authorities, but again, there might be circumstances in which it's morally permissible, even morally obligatory, to disobey. Catholicism does not, however, have this flexibility with regard to all rules of morality. For example, murder (that is, the intentional killing of an innocent human being) is always wrong — no exceptions. And there are many other rules that do not admit of exceptions, that apply to *intrinsic* evils: one must never commit suicide, one must never commit abortion, one must never engage in acts of adultery or fornication or homosexuality; and the list goes on.

Catholicism, in short, has a long list of moral rules that are exceptionless or *absolute*. From this flows the traditional principle: do no evil, even if good might come of it. Suppose this (fortunately far-fetched) dilemma were posed to a Catholic: "If an alien civilization from a distant galaxy threatened to destroy the planet Earth and everything on it unless you consented to violate one of these absolute rules, what would be the morally correct thing to do: violate the rule, or allow the Earth to perish?" From a Catholic point of view, the correct answer would be: "Allow the Earth to perish."

Secularists are not absolutists; if we take the word *relativism* to be the opposite of *absolutism*, they are moral relativists. Theirs is a very flexible system of morality; there can be an exception to any rule. This follows very logically from their subjectivism, for if all moral rules are nothing but man-made creations, then man can simply amend or suspend them at will. Society can change its rules, or the individual can replace society's rules with his own.

Sex

Many of the moral disagreements between Catholicism[35] and secularism, quite obviously, have to do with matters pertaining to sexuality: fornication, cohabitation, divorce, abortion, homosexuality, and so forth. Why should there be so many disagreements on matters of *this* kind? After all, Catholics and secularists don't disagree on the morality of murder or the morality of bank robbery

[35] In this chapter I'll be speaking of disagreements between secularism and *Catholicism*, but it goes without saying that many, although not quite all, of these disagreements also hold between secularism and traditional Protestantism.

or the morality of a hundred other things. Why, then, should they so violently disagree on the morality of sex?

The answer is to be found in the contrasting Catholic and secularist worldviews discussed above. These conflicting worldviews lead quite logically to two different attitudes toward sex. The secularist, who believes that we have only one life to live, a life that will last less than a century out of an infinity of time, sees sex as one of the great opportunities for enjoyment available to him. This isn't to say that secularists are libertines. The great majority of them believe in a certain degree of sexual restraint; after all, an imprudently conducted sex life can lead to all kinds of problems. But so long as prudence is observed, the secularist would argue, we should be quite free to indulge our wishes for sexual enjoyment. In a brief lifetime, why do otherwise?

And it isn't simply a matter of enjoyment, but a matter of experiencing personal relationships and personal growth as well. Without intimate personal relationships, what would life be? Sex can be a shortcut to this intimacy, or a means of deepening an already existing intimacy. Why would any rational man or woman refuse it? Further, why restrict ourselves to a single such intimacy? Downright promiscuity might be imprudent and immature, but a certain amount of sexual diversity, especially in the years of early adulthood, makes good sense to the secularist. These sexual relationships contribute to personal growth. Even relationships that turn out badly make such a contribution, for we can profit even from disappointment and heartache. The person who lives a life of traditional Christian purity, preoccupied with such typically Catholic considerations as marriage, procreation, and genital complementarity, misses out on valuable life lessons.

Catholicism sees sex, like everything created by God, as good in itself, and can agree with the secularist that sex can be a legitimate source of pleasure, intimacy, and personal development. But the Church would add an important qualifier: the utilization of this good thing is rightly reserved, according to Natural Law and divine positive command, to a permanent, exclusive relationship with a single member of the opposite sex, secured by the bonds of marriage. For in the Catholic worldview, even sex has ties to the supernatural world, and in the context of the marriage sacrament, it rises above being a purely natural activity and becomes a supernatural good.

At the same time, the renunciation of all non-marital sex makes good sense according to the Catholic belief in the afterlife. Since our brief lifespan is but a vestibule to eternal life, there's no need to maximize sexual experience and enjoyment (or, for that matter, any other temporal enjoyments and experiences) here below. By renouncing a notable amount of sexual experience here below, we demonstrate, both to others and to ourselves, that we truly believe in the life to come; if we had a merely lip-service belief in a higher world, we wouldn't endorse sexual renunciation.

This is why the life of consecrated celibacy — the life of the monk or nun or priest — has long been considered the ideal Catholic life, the highest calling. Such a life seems pointless from a secularist point of view: what could be more foolish than to throw away all opportunities for sexual experience? But it makes perfect sense for someone who believes that our earthly world, along with its pleasures and its experiences, is as nothing compared with the heavenly world that is our ultimate destiny. What are the sacrifices of a few short years, if they help attain the eternal blessedness of heaven?

And if — as the Church has always affirmed by teaching that the great majority of people are called to the married life — the life of religious celibacy is more than can reasonably be asked of ordinary Catholics, nonetheless the life of the monk or nun or priest can still serve as an example for ordinary Catholics, as though the celibates were saying to them, "We know that you're called to the married state, but let our example remind you to live lives of marital chastity." That is, the life of the ordinary Catholic, while it shouldn't copy the monkish ideal, should at least be inspired by it: inspired to premarital abstinence, to marital fidelity, to avoidance of contraception, and in general to purity of thought, word, and deed. If the Catholic monkish ideal is first-tier Christian sexual renunciation, the Catholic marital ideal is second-tier Christian sexual renunciation.

As for the personal growth that comes, according to the secularist, from a diversity of intimate sexual relationships, Catholics have a twofold answer. One is that they doubt that the multiplication of sexual relationships truly produces genuine intimacy or greater personal growth; more likely, it leads to personal regression and to an impairment of the capacity for intimacy. The other is that pursuit of physical intimacy through multiple sexual partners serves to block the development of spiritual intimacy with God. For most people (with rare exceptions), there seems to be an inverse relationship between the life of prayer and the life of sexual adventure.

Human life

We've looked at sex; let's now turn to the issues of abortion and euthanasia,[36] issues upon which Catholics and secularists differ

[36] When I speak of euthanasia here, I'm using the term in a broad sense, so as to include voluntary and involuntary euthanasia as well as passive and active euthanasia. As I'm using the word, physician-assisted suicide (such as is legally permitted in the state of Oregon) counts as a species of euthanasia.

radically. The contrast here between Catholic and secularist is stark and telling. In making judgments about life issues such as abortion or euthanasia, secularists aren't moved (or at least, if they're logically consistent, *shouldn't* be moved) by the idea that the life of a fetus or a terminally ill person has intrinsic, objective value. From their empiricist-naturalist point of view, such a life can have only whatever "value" might be assigned to it by us humans. If a pregnant woman (assisted, it might be, by her husband or boyfriend and by other friends and relatives, not to mention her doctor and clergy- person) decides that the fetus in her uterus has no value — or, at any rate, a significantly lesser value than other values she's concerned with — it becomes thus. If, on the other hand, she "wants" the child enough, it takes on a completely different value.

Of course, in the case of abortion, the fetus itself has no vote, since it's incapable of having or expressing an opinion. But in the case of euthanasia, the patient ideally has the decisive vote. If, from a secularist viewpoint (i.e., a naturalist-empiricist viewpoint), he decides that his life no longer has value, or at least not enough value to warrant going on, then his life has indeed no value (or relatively small value), and thus, it's morally allowable — even laudable — to terminate it. In cases where the patient's condition has deteriorated to a point at which he's no longer competent to determine the value of his life, then a delegated agent (a close relative or perhaps the doctor) would — presumably in accordance with the patient's own last wishes or his best interests — make that crucial judgment.

The Catholic view is totally different. According to it, the fetus has its *own* value, intrinsic, objective, irrevocable: the value of every human person. Hence, it doesn't matter what subjective value or disvalue anybody — including the mother in whose womb it temporarily resides — might wish to assign to it. Therefore, abortion can't be morally permitted. Neither can euthanasia, whether voluntary or involuntary. It makes no difference whether the person to be killed expresses a clear wish to be killed, since, according to the Catholic view, even if a man expressly wishes to destroy his own life, his objective value as a living human being doesn't vanish thereby. Thus, he may not be killed even at his own request. It follows too that a trustee can't elect to kill an incompetent person, even if he does so in accordance with the person's putative desires or interests. For the human person has not only an objective value, but a very great and absolute value.

That's because, according to the Catholic view, the individual human person is created "in the image and likeness of God" (Gen. 1:26) and thus carries a special dignity that sets him apart from the rest of nature. His human soul is immaterial, made not by any biological process but created directly by God, and so it won't cease to exist with the death of the material body. According to the doctrine of the Incarnation, so high was the value of this body-soul composite made in God's image that it wasn't unworthy of the Second Person of the Trinity to become human; and by taking human nature to himself, God in turn elevated it even further.[37] Finally, Christ's death in the flesh freed humanity from sin and made it possible for all of us to be eternal partakers of God's divine glory. Believing all this, and recognizing (as a point of biological fact) that the fetus, from the moment of conception, is one of

[37] As St. Athanasius wrote in his *On the Incarnation*, "You know how it is when some great king enters a large city and dwells in one of its houses; because of his dwelling in that single house, the whole city is honored . . . . Even so is it with the King of all; He has come into our country and dwelt in one body. . . ."

these wonderful, grand, and noble things called a human person, how can a Catholic rate abortion as anything less than a tremendous evil? Likewise, how can the Catholic rate euthanasia as anything but a tremendous evil?

In fairness to the secularists, it must be acknowledged that, in their own fashion, the great majority of secularists also confer a very high value upon human nature and individual human beings. (At least this is true of present-day American secularists. It wasn't at all true, of course, of earlier secularists of the Nazi or Communist persuasion.) They can be just as shocked and outraged as Christians, often even more so, at certain great injustices and crimes against mankind. Secularists are as eager as Christians, and in many cases more eager, to end or reduce war, poverty, disease, malnutrition, racism, sexism, ignorance, tyranny, and other conditions that are incompatible with the great value and dignity of human beings. It isn't surprising that many of them, given their high regard for humanity, like to call themselves "humanists."

But as we've seen, the typical and logically consistent secularist deems all values to be subjective, the products of our collective or individual value preferences. His superstructure of ethical judgments, including his affinity for human beings, has no sure foundation. And so, at a particular moment in human history (the early twenty-first century) and at a particular place on the planet (the United States of America), the typical secularist might well have a high respect for the worth and dignity of the human person. But the creator of this subjective value can make exceptions (as he does today to allow for abortion and euthanasia), and he's also free to alter his preferences radically: so it's not impossible that someday, perhaps soon, he might decide that only those humans have value who are young and healthy, or sane, or productive, or not overtly religious. I don't say that this *will* happen. I just say that there's nothing in the subjectivist theory of value and morality that must prevent it from happening.

The value of suffering

Secularism, concerned with life in this world only, and rejecting the idea of a future life that might compensate for the sufferings of this life, sees suffering as useless, pointless, indeed the greatest possible evil. Conversely, Catholics believe that the suffering and death of Jesus was the most useful thing that ever happened in the history of the world, since it healed the breach between man and God that had opened with the fall of Adam and Eve. The crucifix, that instrument of ancient Roman cruelty, is the most common of all Catholic symbols; and the principal form of Catholic worship, the Mass, re-enacts the Passion (suffering) and death of Jesus.

From this it follows that if Catholics are to live in imitation of Christ, they're called on to suffer, and to suffer greatly — or at least to be ready and willing to suffer greatly when and if the need arises. The Catholic Church teaches that the connection between our suffering and Christ's goes beyond mere imitation: it has a mystical quality. St. Paul spoke of his own suffering as filling up "what was lacking in the afflictions of Christ" (Col. 1:24). This comes very near to saying that the Christian who suffers voluntarily participates in the redemptive suffering of Christ — that he becomes (to use a theologically controversial phrase) a kind of "co-redeemer" with Christ.

This isn't to say that Catholicism teaches that we must be indifferent to suffering, especially the suffering of others. Far from it. The Gospels are full of stories about Jesus feeding the hungry, curing the sick, giving sight to the blind, serving the poor, casting out demons, even raising the dead. The history of Christianity abounds with corporal works of mercy. What other group has done as much to feed, clothe, shelter, educate, and comfort other human beings as have Christian believers of the last two millennia? It can even be argued that one of the motives that lay behind the scientific revolution that swept the European world in the sixteenth and seventeenth centuries was a desire to get control of nature to ameliorate the bodily and material condition of the human race, and that this desire could have arisen only in a Christian culture, with its strong tradition of works of mercy.

Nonetheless, that's only to point out that Christianity is extremely broad (some might say paradoxically so) in its aims. For however important might be the universal Christian call to ease the temporal suffering of others, the willingness to accept suffering as something meaningful — if suffering is what God has willed for us — is at least equally important. Catholicism is a religion of Christ; hence, it's a religion of the Cross. For this reason Catholics, in fact, not only strive to bear suffering, but also may deliberately seek it out. In the season of Lent, for example, the Catholic is supposed to embrace a certain degree of self-denial, through fasting, abstinence, and selfless labors. And mortification of the flesh — including the intentional self-infliction of small and sometimes great physical discomforts — has been a central value in the monastic tradition since its earliest centuries.

The secularist view of suffering couldn't be more different. If, in the secularist approach to life, there's a certain amount of "active hedonism" (the pursuit of pleasure), there's an even larger amount of what may be called "passive hedonism" (the avoidance of pain). The great prohibition of moral liberalism — namely, "Do not harm non-consenting others" — illustrates this attitude of passive hedonism. If I must not inflict pain on *others*, why should I allow myself to suffer avoidable pain? (Except perhaps in those cases in which pain to myself is an inevitable byproduct of pursuing some other good — for example, the pain of strenuous physical exercise for the sake of good health, or the pain that accompanies hard work done for the benefit of others.) Secularists will grant that suffering is often unavoidable, but they'll never grant that it can be a positive good. The less pain and suffering in the world, the better — *period*. Motivated by this conviction, secularists have often made valuable contributions toward lessening the world's suffering. This explains why most of them would hold that compassion is the second greatest virtue, the greatest, of course, being tolerance.

The Catholic observes a strict prohibition against suicide and euthanasia, regardless of the suffering he or others might be enduring. But from the secularist point of view, it makes little or no sense for a terminally ill person to bear his suffering until the bitter end. If such a person wished to be euthanized, this would be a perfectly rational, even a praiseworthy choice — a triumph of human freedom. And if the dying person were no longer capable of making a choice, it would be rational for his trustees to choose euthanasia for him. Why prolong needless suffering? Here we have the flip side of the secularist's attitude toward sex: just as there's no reason not to maximize pleasure in our short passage through earthly life, so there's no reason to prolong pain.

The Catholic ideally views end-of-life suffering, so far from being pointless, as an opportunity to serve God and, through God, our fellow humans; as such, it's a kind of privilege God allows us. To suffer willingly is to imitate Christ, and not merely to imitate his good works in "those little, nameless, unremembered acts of kindness and of love," which, according to Wordsworth, make up the "best portion of a good man's life," but to imitate — in fact somehow to unite with mystically — the suffering of his Passion and death. This kind of "meritorious" suffering must be borne voluntarily — no Catholic is duty-bound to deny himself or others the full benefits of palliative care — and with a certain prayerful docility of spirit.[38]

These contrasting views of suffering bear not only on end-of-life issues, but on the question of abortion as well. Although secularists hold that the "right to choose" is an absolute right that can be exercised for any reason and not just for a "good" reason, nonetheless when publicly defending abortion, they usually cite hard cases to dramatize their point — cases in which carrying and caring for the baby would be very burdensome for the mother. Why, they ask, should she have to endure this pointless suffering?

Catholics don't have to deny that the baby might be a great burden to the mother, while insisting, of course, that no mere burden gives one the right to kill someone else. What they would deny is that her suffering need be pointless. Its meaning might not be immediately apparent, but, provided the burden is accepted in the right spirit, it might well turn out to be meaningful — to the mother, to other people, and to God. Consider the case of a mother who chooses to keep a baby who, prenatal tests show, will almost certainly be seriously retarded. To the secularist, the suffering that the mother will have to endure in taking care of a seriously and hopelessly disabled child (not to mention the suffering the child would have to endure throughout his life) is hard or impossible to justify. Yet, as countless cases have shown, if she embraces that suffering with an attitude of love, the mother can come to see her child as among the most precious gifts from God. The child can live to be a witness to God's goodness and a mother's love.

[38] The late Pope John Paul II provided such an example in his later years, as he bore, publicly and with apparently a great deal of patience, humility, and prayer, the great physical infirmities that befell him.

And so the gap between Catholicism and secularism is no small one. It can't be ignored, set aside, papered over, or bridged by compromise. It's a gap between diametrically opposite views of reality: one naturalistic, the other supernaturalistic. It's a gap between opposing theories of knowledge: one strictly empiricist, the other allowing for trans-empirical knowledge. It's a gap between two moralities: a largely objective, absolute morality hostile toward fornication, cohabitation, homosexual conduct, abortion, and euthanasia, versus a subjective, mostly relativistic morality favorable toward all those things. It is, in sum, the gap between the City of God and the City of Man, and between these two there is a great gulf fixed: if one of them is right, the other is wrong.

No wonder, then, that there's a Culture War raging between them; each side is fighting furiously for its cultural life. If one side comes to dominate American society, the other will be pushed into the shade. The losing side won't necessarily vanish from America (although it might), but it will be consigned to the margins of American society; it will become a hole-in-the-corner thing. Neither side, of course, wants this to happen to itself, and each would be very pleased to see it happen to the other. For this reason, when the principles and allegiances of each side are laid bare, who can be surprised when Catholics — that is, Catholics of the orthodox variety — abandon the Democratic Party, the party that has become the ally and instrument of anti-Catholic secularism?

Chapter 5

Catholic Excuses

Nonetheless, even today great numbers of Catholics continue to support the Democratic Party despite its strong commitment to the anti-Christian agenda of secularism and moral liberalism. If the party has become so palpably the enemy of their religion, how can this be? How can Catholics justify tearing down with their political left hand what they build up with their religious right hand? How do they reconcile things that are apparently irreconcilable? How can they be both Democrat and Catholic without suffering sharp pains of cognitive dissonance?

The methods by which Catholic Democrats commonly accomplish this tend to fall into one of several categories that I'll now explore. In so doing I'll focus almost exclusively on the question of abortion, omitting any discussion of homosexuality, euthanasia, and so forth. I'll limit myself in this way, first, for economy's sake — why make the chapter any longer than it has to be? But another reason is that the argument over abortion has been going on for so long that by now the Catholic excuses for supporting it are old hat and very well known; this isn't quite so true for Catholic defenses of homosexuality, euthanasia, and so on. Besides, it's likely that the justifications for homosexuality, euthanasia, and other such issues will in the end be pretty much the same justifications, *mutatis mutandis*, that have been used over the past few decades to justify Catholic support for a pro-abortion politics.

Catholic excuses start with Catholic leadership

Before looking at the specific excuses by which lay Catholic voters and politicians justify their support for a secularist Democratic Party, it should be noted that there would be fewer such excuses — and fewer Catholic Democrats — were it not for certain failures on the part of the clergy. Many American bishops and pastors have been ineffective at communicating to their people the unequivocal Catholic teaching on abortion and other Culture War issues. Likewise they've been ineffective at dissuading Catholic politicians from supporting items on the secularist moral agenda. Needless to say, there have been notable exceptions; but by and large, the leadership given by bishops in the last thirty or forty years to the American Church has been marked by weakness: in oversight of catechesis and liturgy, in seminary formation, in discipline of clergy and of high-profile dissenters in politics and higher education, and in providing a clear, authoritative voice in those often-murky areas where religion and politics intersect.

Many priests too are guilty of timidity, fearful of giving offense to certain persons in the pews by sermonizing against abortion or homosexuality. They don't seem to realize that although such a sermon might offend a small number of parishioners, it would be welcomed — perhaps even applauded — by a great majority. For although it's true that many self-identified Catholics are sympathetic, for example, to abortion rights, these aren't usually the same ones to be found in church on Sundays. As I argued in my book *The Decline and Fall of the Catholic Church in America*, the clergy would do well to change the way they "count" Catholics, focusing first on the regular churchgoers, and adapt their ministry accordingly.

Many priests, and perhaps some bishops, fail to lead in the fight against Catholicism's secularist enemies in part because they have a kind of sympathy with them. For instance, they might see feminism as an admirable struggle for social justice; they might consider the gay movement a worthwhile struggle for human rights. They usually don't support the more unfortunate components of these movements — few, for example, are unabashedly pro-choice — yet they won't speak against abortion. Many of these priests with a strong "social justice" orientation tend, like their lay counterparts, to sympathize with the Democratic Party, which they perceive as the political party with the stronger historical record of battling for social justice. This partisan sympathy makes them reluctant to treat the party as an enemy in the Culture War no matter how much its agenda opposes Church teaching.

A good percentage of these priests come from the generation ordained in the late 1960s through the '70s. Their formation, which took place during a time of both cultural and religious upheaval marked by a generalized rejection of authority, left many of them with a disdain for old-fashioned Catholicism; they came out as religious progressives, a bit soft in their orthodoxy. And at the same time, many were finding elements of *secular* progressivism attractive. Because of age, priests of this generation are now beginning to pass from the scene, but for decades they've been the dominant force in the American Catholic clergy.

Thanks in part to the priest shortage, few or virtually none of even the worst priests — the most timid, the most uninformed, the most sympathetic to cultural liberalism — ever find themselves severely corrected by their bishops, who, if nothing else, are loath to lose a priest by acting in too "authoritarian" a manner.

Also, like all big corporations, a diocesan chancery is a bureaucratic place, today more so than ever before. A bishop must follow procedures, listen to committee recommendations, delegate tasks. He has less direct knowledge and less hands-on control of his diocese today than he would have had in the old days. So no matter how orthodox a bishop might be, if he's overwhelmed by financial and legal matters and surrounded, as he often is, by layers of more or less liberal staff, he'll be less effective at disciplining his priests and at teaching and guiding his lay flock.

Perhaps the most prevalent reasons for the clergy's failure to lead in these areas is also the simplest: many bishops and priests seem to be simply ignorant of the menace that secularism poses to their religion. They would recognize anti-Christianity if it took the form of outright persecution, as it used to do in the Communist countries of Central and Eastern Europe and as it does in China and Cuba today. But they don't recognize the sociological signs of the more subtle, and perhaps more effective, form it currently takes in the United States.

More perhaps than any other Christian denomination, the Catholic Church is a bishop-and-priest-dominated religion (a "priest-ridden" religion, some would say). When clerical leadership is strong and wise, the quality of lay Catholicism will be high. But when clerical leadership is weak or foolish, we can't be surprised when the quality of lay Catholicism sinks. Such times help give rise to those common "excuses" we will now examine.

THE DENOMINATIONAL MENTALITY:
" *'Thinking for myself' is more important than dogma.*"

In the course of the nineteenth and twentieth centuries, American Catholics of European descent gradually Americanized, and as they did so, they adopted what has become the dominant

American attitude toward religion: what may be called the denominational mentality (DM) — a synonym for which is the old-fashioned and too-cumbersome word *latitudinarianism*. Unlike sects and churches of the old-fashioned kind, which tend to be strongly dogmatic in their belief systems, the kind of religious organizations that I'm calling "denominations" tend to be theologically tolerant and un-dogmatic. Members of churches of the denominational type (the mainline Protestant churches — Episcopal, Methodist, Presbyterian, American Baptist, United Church of Christ, and so forth) de-emphasize the dogmatic aspects of religion. They don't think any the worse of you if you happen to disagree with the tenets of their faith. The important thing, as they see it, is that you're a morally decent person and that you have *some* religious faith, but which faith it is doesn't particularly matter. This is the mentality — a mentality of *creedal and theological tolerance* above all — that I have in mind when I speak of the DM.

For a long time Catholics in America, under strong and decisive clerical leadership (I refer here not just to bishops but to priests and teaching nuns as well), resisted the temptation to adopt the DM. They insisted, rather to the annoyance of their DM Protestant neighbors, that the Catholic religion was the one true Faith; that their Catholic Church was the one true Church of Jesus Christ.

But in the 1960s all of this changed. It changed partly from the influence of Vatican II, which, while not renouncing the "one true Faith" claim, dropped the emphatically anti-Protestant tone that had characterized the Catholic Church since the Reformation in the sixteenth century. Partly too it changed because Catholics, who had long been second-class Americans in a strongly Protestant country, finally came into their own as first-class Americans; the election of John Kennedy to the White House symbolized this arrival. By 1970 American Catholics had pretty much let their "one true Faith" claim lapse. Their attitude had become the DM. For most practical purposes, Catholicism had become one more mainline Protestant religion.[39]

The application among Catholics of this denominational mentality soon spread, as it had among mainline Protestants, from theological dogmas to moral doctrines. Not only did you no longer have to believe in a virgin birth or miracles or damnation, but as long as you were a decent person with *some* religious affiliation, it didn't really matter if you violated certain traditional Christian moral taboos; it was up to your personal conscience whether you wanted to fornicate, or divorce, or have an abortion. Even if you weren't a religious believer at all, as long as you were a decent person, you could decide such moral questions for yourself — according to your conscience rather than some religious authority.

I certainly don't contend that all Catholics adopted the DM. But by the 1970s it had been adopted in some measure, often in large measure, by the vast numbers of American Catholics.[40] It's no surprise that Catholics of this kind should feel no cognitive

[39] For a fuller treatment of this concept of the DM, see my book *The Decline and Fall of the Catholic Church in America,* especially chapters 13 through 19.

[40] Some will argue that DM Catholics are Catholic in name only. How can a person be a member in good standing of this highly dogmatic religion when he dismisses dogma as a thing of little or no consequence? Since this book isn't a work of theology, I won't try to decide the theological question of whether these virtual non-believers should count as Catholics. Rather, it's a work of sociology, and sociologically speaking we must count such people as Catholic as long as they call themselves Catholic and nobody in a position of authority has excommunicated them.

dissonance when voting for pro-choice candidates or when supporting the Democratic Party generally. What does it matter to them that their Church condemns abortion or homosexual activity? The pope might feel that these things are wrong, and the pope is certainly entitled to his opinion; but why should they have to agree with that opinion? While they consider themselves Catholic, they're the kind of Catholics who "think for themselves," and they've come to the honest conclusion that in some circumstances abortion and homosexuality are morally permissible. And so, of course, they're not in the least troubled by the Democratic Party's endorsement of these practices. As they see it, that the party supports moral liberalism is one of its great merits.

BLISSFUL IGNORANCE: *"Culture War? What Culture War?"*

Many Catholic Democrats have never even considered that there might be an incompatibility between their political and religious identities. And I don't refer only to those who are no more than nominal Catholics — the kind of people who were baptized and perhaps brought up Catholic but now as adults rarely darken a church door. You'd expect people like that to feel no cognitive dissonance about supporting a secularist agenda. But in this category too are Catholics who take their religion seriously and never fail to go to Mass on a weekend. It's no doubt true that by now many regular Catholic churchgoers, if they were Democrats in the first place, have abandoned the party. But many remain, so many, in fact, that, if it weren't for them, the Democratic Party would be far worse off than it is now.

For these people, being both a Catholic and a Democrat has never been problematic. They've been Catholics ever since they were baptized as infants, and they've been Democrats for as long as they can remember; their parents were Catholic Democrats before them, and so were their grandparents. It's a family trait.[41]

But how can this be — that a serious, practicing Catholic will also be a serious, practicing Democrat? Can a Catholic be unaware of the Church's condemnation of abortion, or can a Democrat be unaware of the party's commitment to the cause of abortion rights? Can a Catholic be unaware of the Church's condemnation of homosexual conduct, or can a Democrat be unaware of the party's growing commitment to same-sex marriage? The short answer to these questions is: Yes, people can be unaware of these things, and many actually are.

Although the Democratic Party's pro-abortion commitment is no secret to anybody who's paying attention, not everybody pays attention, especially when paying attention can involve such things as examining voting records in the U.S. Senate and House and scrutinizing contributions made to political candidates by pro-choice PACs and individuals. Let's say you're sixty years old or more, you're a Democrat, you're a Catholic, and you're pro-life. I don't mean *ardently* pro-life: you're not the kind of person who pickets at abortion clinics, or even the kind who occasionally mails a check to a pro-life organization; but as a Catholic, you

[41] When I was growing up in Rhode Island, for instance, you could take it for granted that if a person was Catholic and Irish, he'd almost certainly be a Democrat. It wasn't unheard of that an Italian Catholic would be a Republican. This was the result of an old antagonism between the Irish and the Italians; for a long time the Irish, having arrived in America first, monopolized city-hall patronage, giving Italians little more than crumbs from the table, thereby pushing many of them into Republican arms. But even Italians were far more likely to be Democrats than Republicans.

have no doubt that abortion is seriously wrong. Your friends and fellow parishioners are pretty much like you: earnest Catholics, lifelong Democrats, opposed to abortion, and not particularly interested in following every development in national politics. When Democratic candidates for the U.S. House or Senate turn up to speak to folks of your kind, they don't emphasize their pro-abortion and pro-gay credentials; in fact, if possible, they avoid the topics of abortion and homosexuality. Instead they talk about social security, health care, education for your grandchildren, getting rid of the potholes in the roads, and so on. They save their pro-abortion speeches for fundraisers attended by supporters of Planned Parenthood and the ACLU. So how are you to know that the national Democratic Party is strongly committed to abortion rights?

Likewise you can be relatively ignorant of the Church's strong opposition to abortion and same-sex marriage. You're aware, of course, that the Church is in some sense opposed to these things, but how seriously opposed? The Church, to take another case, is also opposed to contraception. But that mustn't be a big deal, you (along with millions of others) figure, because the Church rarely or never makes an issue of it. Everybody knows that most Catholic married couples practice contraception, including — to judge from the smallness of their families — most of the younger couples you see in your parish church at weekend Masses. Yet priests rarely or never fulminate against contraception when giving sermons. Never mind fulminate — almost no priest ever utters a peep on the topic.[42] You might reasonably conclude that the Church, despite

[42] The only time I remember hearing contraception mentioned from the pulpit was when I was young boy, about ten years old, in the late 1940s. And even then I didn't hear a sermon on the subject. Instead I heard the priest say that he would *not* be giving a sermon about "birth

its *pro forma* disapproval, doesn't really consider contraception a big deal. What, then, does the relative pulpit silence about abortion signify? And what does the almost complete silence about homosexuality signify?[43]

The average Catholic Democrat in the pew can hardly be blamed for concluding that the Church is barely more serious about abortion and homosexuality than it is about contraception. And since he might well be unaware of his party's rooted commitment to the tenets of moral liberalism, he's able to carry on without cognitive dissonance, in blissful ignorance remaining a faithful member of two opposed and irreconcilable communities.

TENACITY:
"Don't trouble me with the facts."

The name for this "method" was wittily coined by the nineteenth-century American philosopher Charles Sanders Peirce, who described the practice of it in these terms: It's done by "taking any answer to a question which we may fancy, and constantly reiterating it to ourselves, dwelling on all which may conduce to that belief, and learning to turn with contempt and hatred from anything which might disturb it."[44]

control" because of the presence of children in the pews. It sticks in memory because I didn't understand what birth control was or why it was something unsuitable for little ears. Children, it seems, had very delicate ears in those far-off days.

43 Not all pulpits are silent on the topic of homosexuality. Some priests use an occasional homily to remind the faithful that, as Christians, they have a special duty to be kind to gays and lesbians.

44 This is from Peirce's famous essay, "The Fixation of Belief" (1877), which can be found reprinted in many

This is the "method" used by the betrayed wife who at some level of consciousness knows that her husband has been cheating, but forces the idea out of her mind. If she thinks too much about it, unpleasant consequences might follow; better, then, to pretend it never happened. And this is exactly the mental game played by Catholic Democrats who know in their heart of hearts that their political and religious affiliations are incompatible, but would like to pretend they're not. For if they face up to this conflict, they'll have to deal with it, and that would be unpleasant. It would be especially unpleasant if they were Democratic candidates or office-holders, even at the most humble level; for it might lead to a change of career. But even for ordinary Democratic voters it would be unpleasant, since it's never easy to deal with the possibility of having to renounce an old habit, and it's even less easy to have to renounce a comfortable identity. So they feel the cognitive dissonance but try to repress it; they cling tenaciously to *both* identities — Catholic and Democrat — and stubbornly refuse to discuss, either with others or with themselves, their incompatibility.

THE POLITICIAN'S EXCUSE:
"I'm personally opposed, but . . ."

There's a very large class of Catholic Democratic politicians[45] who fall into the "I'm personally opposed to abortion but . . ." category. Two of their favorite excuses are these:

> "I have a duty to represent *all* my constituents, not just the Catholic ones."

places, including Philip P. Weiner, ed., *Charles S. Peirce: Selected Writings* (New York: Dover Books, 1958), 101.

[45] See Appendix V for a more thorough look at this excuse and its most famous exponent.

> "I've taken a solemn oath to support and defend the Constitution of the United States. In *Roe v. Wade* the U.S. Supreme Court has declared that abortion is a constitutionally protected right. Therefore, it's my duty to support and defend the right to abortion." What this last sentence means for them in practice is this: "It's my solemn duty under the U.S. Constitution to vote against bans on partial-birth abortion, to vote in favor of taxpayer funding of abortion, and to do all I can to block presidential nominations to the Supreme Court of justices who might turn out to be anti-*Roe*."

The validity of both these excuses is easily demolished by comparing them with analogous excuses that might have been given sixty or more years ago for supporting racial segregation — so easily demolished, in fact, that we might be surprised to learn that otherwise very intelligent politicians would resort to such lame excuses. (At least we *would* be surprised if we weren't aware of how powerful the passion of political ambition can be. It's often powerful enough to render logical politicians illogical and intellectually honest politicians dishonest.) What would our pro-choice Catholic politicians have thought of an alibi that ran as follows?

> "I have a duty to represent *all* my constituents, not just Negroes. I'm duty-bound to represent my racist constituents too, and they favor a regime of white supremacy. Personally, I'm opposed to racism, but . . ."

And what would our pro-choice Catholic politician have thought of an excuse along the following lines?

> "I've taken a solemn oath to support and defend the Constitution of the United States. In *Plessey v. Ferguson* the U.S.

Supreme Court has declared that racial segregation is a constitutionally protected practice. Therefore, it's my duty to support and defend the institution of racial segregation." What this last sentence would mean in practice was: "It's my solemn duty under the U.S. Constitution to vote against bans on lynch law and to work to maintain Negro disenfranchisement, racially segregated schools, and racially segregated units in the U.S. military. To cave in on any of these things would be a grave violation of my oath of office, which I take very seriously."

THE PRIMACY OF CONSCIENCE: *"Nothing is right or wrong, but thinking makes it so."*

On February 28, 2006, fifty-five Catholic Democrats from the U.S. House of Representatives signed on to a "Statement of Principles" released with the headline: "House Democrats Release Historic Catholic Statement of Principles. — Expresses Commitment to Dignity of Life and Belief that Government Has 'Moral Purpose.' "

The Statement of Principles declared, "We . . . agree with the Catholic Church about the value of human life and the undesirability of abortion; we do not celebrate its practice." Who knew that this was the Catholic position — that abortion is "undesirable," that it isn't something you want to "celebrate"? Haven't the honorable members heard that the Catholic Church considers abortion to be an act of unwarranted homicide?

The statement then goes on to say, "We seek the Church's guidance and assistance but believe also in the primacy of conscience. In recognizing the Church's role in providing moral leadership, we acknowledge and accept the tension that comes with being in disagreement with the Church in some areas." The expression "being in disagreement with the Church in some areas" is, of course, extremely ambiguous. Does it refer to disagreement on matters of fundamental Church teaching (e.g., the Resurrection) — the kind of disagreement that makes a person, technically speaking, a heretic? Or does it refer only to disagreements with Church leaders on questions of practical policy — the way, say, a Catholic might disagree with the pope's opinion on whether or not Turkey should be admitted to the EU? There's a very big difference between the two.

In view of the statement's assertion that abortion is "undesirable" and not something to cheer about, it appears that the disagreement referred to here has to do with the Church's teaching on abortion. But that's a fundamental teaching, not just a policy preference: the Church's teaching on abortion is far closer to its teaching on the Resurrection than it is to the pope's wish to keep Turkey out of the EU.

And then there is "the primacy of conscience." This too is an ambiguous expression. There's one sense in which this phrase has a very legitimate Catholic meaning in traditional Catholic moral theology, but another sense — a very popular one in present-day America, it must be granted — in which it does not.

The traditional Catholic teaching is that we must always act in accordance with conscience: "A human being must always obey the certain judgment of his conscience."[46] But prior to that, we must make an honest effort to form a *correct* conscience, in part by studying and heeding the teachings of the Church. If, after making an honest attempt to form a correct conscience, we happen to form an erroneous conscience, and in following that conscience do something that objectively violates the moral law, we would

[46] *Catechism of the Catholic Church*, no. 1790.

nonetheless be subjectively without blame. According to this legitimate idea of conscience, conscience isn't the ultimate moral authority, but rather our closest contact with it; that by which we gauge whether we're acting in conformity with right and wrong. Thus, our conscience is authoritative only insofar as we've made an honest effort to form it according to the ultimate moral authority: the Law of God, which all human beings perceive as the Natural Law.[47]

According to the other, popular idea of conscience, our conscience is the supreme or ultimate authority in moral matters. Conscience of this kind disregards Natural Law or divine positive law, and it trumps the teaching of any church or religion, including the Catholic Church. In this view of conscience, as in the other view, there's a place for honesty.

But here it isn't the honesty involved in an attempt to conform our judgment to the moral law or to the ethical teachings of the Church. Rather it's a matter of being honest with ourselves. We have to answer the question, "Do I honestly *feel* that this is the

[47] For an account of the Catholic idea of conscience and its authority, see the *Catechism of the Catholic Church*, nos. 1776-1794. Or see Thomas Aquinas, *Summa Theologica*, I-II, Q. 19, arts. 5 and 6. Or see John Henry Newman's "Conscience" chapter in his *Letter to the Duke of Norfolk* (Newman's reply to Gladstone's criticism of the decrees of the First Vatican Council). Newman, although a great believer in papal authority, was not one to slight the authority of conscience; yet he certainly wouldn't have applauded the Statement of Principles. He closes the "Conscience" chapter with this famous remark: "Certainly, if I am obliged to bring religion into after-dinner toasts (which indeed does not seem quite the thing), I shall drink — to the Pope, if you please — still, to Conscience first, and to the Pope afterwards."

right thing to do?" If the answer to this question is yes, then in doing it, we're acting in accordance with conscience and thus acting morally.

Take, for example, a Catholic member of Congress who's confronted with a bill that would use taxpayer money to pay for abortions. According to the first idea of conscience, the member would consult the Natural Law and conclude that a yes vote on this bill would be immoral; and he would consult the teachings of the Church and discover the same thing. Accordingly his conscience, now well formed, would tell him to vote no, and if he, in fact, voted no, he'd be acting in obedience to conscience. But according to the second idea of conscience, he'd ask himself before voting, "Do I honestly feel that a yes vote on this bill would be the right thing to do?" If he honestly felt this, then a yes vote on this bill would be in accordance with his conscience — regardless of Natural Law or the very clear and explicit teachings of the Church; and so he would vote yes.

And of course, since average human nature has a great capacity for self-deception, this Catholic politician will find that his "honest" feelings can be strongly influenced by those who hold the key to his political future. He won't heed Natural Law or the pronouncements of popes, but he will heed the wishes of his constituents — and especially the wishes of his major campaign contributors.

Cardinal Newman held that the voice of conscience was the voice of God within us.[48] It's obvious, then, that Newman never had the privilege of meeting a twenty-first-century Catholic Democratic member of Congress. For if he had, he would have realized

[48] See John Henry Newman's *Grammar of Assent*, the "Belief in One God" section.

that sometimes the "voice of conscience" is the voice of ideologues, usually those with deep pockets.

THE "SEAMLESS GARMENT":
"We must be concerned with all life issues."

Another method Catholics use to validate their membership in the Democratic Party, despite the party's anti-Christian moral agenda, goes like this: they concede that abortion, for example, is morally wrong and that it's tragically wrong for the Democratic Party to support it; but then they talk about the need for "balance" and the importance of not taking a single-issue approach to politics. "The Democrats," they say, "might be wrong on a few issues, such as abortion and same-sex marriage — but they're right about so many other important issues: race, poverty, peace, education, health care, the environment, and so on. In politics we have to weigh in the balance the evil and the good, and in the Democratic Party it turns out that the good greatly outweighs the evil. If there were a major political party that took the correct stands on *every* important issue, then we Catholics would support it. But no such party exists, and in this bent world of sin and error no such party is ever likely to exist. So we have to do the best we can."

"A loyal Catholic," these Democratic apologists continue, "is tempted, of course, to become a single-issue politician or voter and to base political choices purely on the abortion issue. This temptation is understandable, given the dreadful nature of abortion as seen through Catholic eyes; but it must be resisted. Mature citizens of a mature democracy realize that there's always more than one issue at stake. Abortion is a terrible evil, to be sure, but it's far from being the *only* evil; it's but one front in the battle against the world's manifold evil. If we were to concentrate all our efforts there, we might — just might — win a victory, but we would assure ourselves of being defeated everywhere else along the line; and if we lost everywhere else, we would probably eventually lose on the abortion front as well. Let us, then, do our best to fight the entire battle, and this means allying ourselves with the Democratic Party, with which we have so many values and aims in common."

This kind of argument acquired a certain degree of respectability in Catholic circles about twenty years ago because it bore a resemblance — a deceptive resemblance, I argue — to the "seamless garment" or "consistent ethic of life" position put forward by the late Cardinal Joseph Bernardin, Archbishop of Chicago. In an address ("A Consistent Ethic of Life: An American-Catholic Dialogue") delivered at Fordham University in New York City on December 6, 1983, Bernardin too rejected the notion that Catholics should adopt a single-issue approach to politics, even if that single issue happened to be abortion. He asserted that Catholic opposition to abortion should be part of a larger pro-life package. Catholics, he said, should also be opposed to poverty, disease, racism, and so on, because all these things are at odds with the sanctity of life.

Bernardin was speaking about six months after the Catholic bishops of the United States had issued their ground-breaking pastoral letter *The Challenge of Peace*, in which they reflected on the moral limits of America's nuclear-deterrence theory. The letter was drawn up under Bernardin's leadership; he was the chairman of the committee charged with drafting it. In his Fordham speech he argued that an attitude of respect for the "sacredness of human life" must underlie Catholic views on war, abortion, and even capital punishment. He went on to say:

> If one contends, as we [Catholics] do, that the right of every fetus to be born should be protected by civil law and

> supported by civil consensus, then our moral, political, and economic responsibilities do not stop at the moment of birth. Those who defend the right to life of the weakest among us must be equally visible in support of the quality of life of the powerless among us: the old and the young, the hungry and the homeless, the undocumented immigrant and the unemployed worker. Such a quality of life posture translates into specific political and economic positions on tax policy, employment generation, welfare policy, nutrition and feeding programs, and health care. Consistency means we cannot have it both ways. We cannot urge a compassionate society and vigorous public policy to protect the rights of the unborn and then argue that compassion and significant public programs on behalf of the needy undermine the moral fiber of the society or are beyond the proper scope of governmental responsibility.

In effect, although not in so many words, Bernardin was suggesting a third political agenda distinct from both the standard liberalism of the Democrats and the standard conservatism of the Republicans. At the moment he made his famous speech, the Democrats were the party of abortion while at the same time having a long tradition of being the "social justice" party. The Republicans, by contrast, were the anti-abortion party, while at the same time being the traditional party of big-money interests and hence less interested in social-justice issues.[49] To Bernardin the

[49] I'm not saying that Republicans have been *completely* uninterested in such issues, just far less interested than post-1932 Democrats. Republicans had a very strong interest in racial-justice issues during the Lincoln administration and throughout the Reconstruction period, for instance, and in the twentieth century there was a significant

Democratic social-justice agenda was gravely deficient without an anti-abortion component. On the other hand, the Republican pro-life agenda was also deficient, lacking a generalized social-justice component — pro-life in a merely truncated fashion, caring much about abortion but relatively little about fighting poverty, racism, sexism, capital punishment, and so on. What was needed, said Bernardin, was an agenda that combined pro-life concerns with (other) social-justice concerns. For all practical purposes, and whether he realized it or not, Bernardin was calling for a new third party in American politics, for it was perfectly clear that neither of the major parties was about to transform itself according to his wishes.

But no third party emerged, although here and there small groups of Catholics, and some non-Catholics, warmly greeted Bernardin's suggestion. For the most part, these were social-justice liberals with a strong traditional attachment to the Democratic Party. They were feeling considerable cognitive dissonance because their pro-life convictions conflicted with their attachment to the increasingly pro-abortion Democratic Party, and Bernardin showed them, or at least *seemed* to show them, a way out of this dilemma. He showed how they could be pro-life while remaining social-justice liberals. Indeed he persuaded them that

Republican tradition of concern — typified by such personalities as Theodore Roosevelt, Robert LaFollette, and Nelson Rockefeller — for the social underdog. It can also be argued with some plausibility that Republicans have done more for the poor by encouraging business than have Democrats with their array of social-justice legislation and government programs. But this doesn't change the fact that a *conscious and deliberate* focus on social-justice questions has been much more of a Democratic characteristic than a Republican characteristic.

they themselves, and not the pro-choice Democrats, were the *true* social-justice liberals.

But no matter how many people found the cardinal's proposals attractive from an abstract and philosophical point of view, it soon became evident that in the real world of politics, people who thought like Bernardin were small in numbers and of virtually no political significance. Sides had already been chosen up, political players already committed. Social-justice liberals, almost all of them Democrats, were either themselves pro-choice or were political bedfellows with the pro-choice movement, and people who were pro-life, almost all of them Republican, were either themselves economic conservatives or were in bed politically with economic conservatives.

At all events, in the end, Bernardin's "consistent ethic of life" proposal came to nothing of significance. Its only lasting consequence can be found in the Catholics who misunderstood it (deliberately, in more than a few cases), invoking the seamless garment to rationalize their support for liberal Democratic politicians. "I'm sorry to have to admit that Sen. X is wrong on abortion," they said, "but please note that he's right on everything else that the late, great Cardinal Bernardin was concerned about: taxes, health care, education, welfare, racism, sexism, war, capital punishment, and anything else you can mention. His consistent ethic-of-life record is eighty or ninety percent — not perfect, but far better than the record of his so-called 'pro-life' Republican opponent."

This superficially persuasive line of reasoning could have been used to support the Nazis in the 1930s.[50] A pro-Nazi Catholic could say, "Oh yes, it's too bad — this policy of the Fuehrer toward

[50] Comparisons are odious, and comparisons involving Nazis doubly so, but the analogy is nonetheless sound.

the Jews. We deplore the firing of Jewish professors, we deplore the Nuremberg laws, we deplore *Kristellnacht*. But anti-Semitism, while a great evil, isn't the only evil. Far from it. We have to balance the evil done by the National Socialists against the good they've accomplished. Hitler has revived the economy, has restored law and order, has built autobahns and Volkswagens, has won the respect and salutary fear of the international community, has once again made it possible for Germans, who had been so humiliated for so long a time, to lift up their heads and be proud of their nation. Hitler isn't perfect — no politician ever will be. The question is, 'Are the Nazis on the whole producing more good than evil? Are they better than the available alternatives — namely, socialists and communists?' The answer to this question is, without doubt, yes."

Somebody might object that my analogy exaggerates the evil of abortion, which surely isn't comparable to anti-Semitism even in its pre-genocidal stage. Yes, "somebody" might say this, but Catholics who understand the moral teaching of their own religion can't very well say it. To them, the forty million and more abortion-homicides that have taken place in the United States since the 1973 *Roe* decision are clearly a greater moral evil than Hitler's pre-genocide anti-Semitism of the 1930s and even, it can be argued, no less an evil than the six million homicides that made up the Holocaust. Some people will scoff at this comparison, but that's simply an indication that they reject the Catholic teaching that abortion is homicide. It's quite understandable that many non-Catholics, especially secularists and moral liberals and liberal religious believers, would reject this teaching. But if you're a Catholic who doesn't reject it, how can you support the Democratic Party, the party of abortion?

One more point. When Bernardin said that abortion isn't the only "life" issue and that there are many others, he didn't say that the abortion was somehow outweighed by other life issues and could therefore be ignored. Bernardin said nothing to suggest that he rejected the traditional Catholic notion that there's a hierarchy of moral evil. Poverty is a bad thing, and so is racism, and so is ill-health; but their badness is not as bad as the badness of directly killing an innocent human person (to say nothing of forty million of them), not even when racism and poverty and ill-health are all added together. In fact, it's hard, from a Catholic point of view, to think of any evil greater than the mass homicide that is abortion — considered both in the scope of its numbers and in proportion to the helplessness of its victims. A logically consistent Catholic would have to rank abortion as the very worst evil afflicting the United States today, worst by a wide margin — the paramount evil.

SOCIAL WELFARE:
"We should be more concerned with children already born."

Often heard as an adjunct to the "seamless garment" excuse is this argument: "You pro-lifers are tremendously concerned about the well-being of the unborn baby, but we notice that you lose interest in the baby once it's born. You don't support daycare, welfare, and other programs that would lead to happier, healthier lives for children. Your pro-life philosophy is inconsistent, and you personally are hypocrites."

Two replies can be made to this charge. First, it's false. When moral conservatives object to social programs such as state-funded daycare and generous welfare payments, it's usually because they believe that such programs ultimately *harm* children by gradually undermining the married two-parent family. Who can deny that the institution of the married two-parent family is better for children than daycare, welfare, and the like? Moral conservatives might not always have the right answers, but they're at least free of hypocrisy when they contend — and not without a serious argument — that they're supporting policies aimed at helping children both unborn *and* born. (And if many of them nonetheless seem much more passionate and vocal about helping the unborn, they can probably be forgiven for responding with a fervor proportionate to the nature of the injustice they perceive.)

If anybody is hypocritical in this discussion, it's moral liberals, who profess to be concerned about kids living in poverty yet endorse the ethic of sexual liberation, which for the last three or four decades has contributed greatly to an epidemic of divorce and out-of-wedlock births, pauperizing women and dooming tens of millions of kids to grow up without fathers.

Second, even if it were true, the charge is beside the point — an example of the *ad hominem* fallacy. That Mr. Jones is a thief doesn't prove that he's in error when he says that bank robbery is immoral. Nor does the hypocrisy of Mrs. Jones prove that she's in error when she says that abortion is wicked.

ANTI-HYPOCRISY:
"Conservatives defy the Church too."

"You fault me as an inconsistent Catholic because I support the Democratic Party," a Catholic Democrat might say to a morally conservative Catholic pro-lifer who has turned against the Democratic Party. "But this is a case of the pot calling the kettle black. *You* favor the war in Iraq and the death penalty, yet both of these are condemned by the Church. In the run-up to the war in early 2003, the late Pope John Paul II made it clear that he favored not war but further diplomatic effort. And for years the pope condemned the death penalty, arguing that in modern nations there's no good reason to use it. So how can you insist that I must strictly conform to the teaching of the Church on one issue, abortion, while at the same time you blithely disregard the Church on two issues?"

Let's leave aside the question of whether John Paul II's calls for peace and diplomacy meant he actually believed the American invasion of Iraq to be immoral. For no matter what he thought about the moral status of the war, who can be surprised that he would make a plea for further diplomacy? Calling for peaceful solutions is one of the things you do if you're pope. In the event he considered the war justified, what was he supposed to do — bless the cruise missiles? In the latter part of the eleventh century, Pope Urban II went to France and called for a crusade to recapture the Holy Land from the Muslim Turks, but today isn't the eleventh century, and popes don't do that kind of thing anymore.

As I said, though, even granting for the sake of argument that the pope judged the Iraq war to be immoral, this judgment isn't a matter of Church doctrine, binding on all Catholics. The Church has a traditional teaching as to what constitutes a "just war," but there has been no definitive dogmatic pronouncement that the Iraq war in particular was an unjust war: the Church doesn't make dogmatic statements about things like that. Some Catholics (perhaps the pope among them) held that the war was unjust by Catholic just-war standards; other Catholics, using the same standards, held that the war was just. To disagree with the pope's putative opinion on the Iraq war doesn't involve rejection of any Catholic doctrine; but to "disagree with the pope" — John Paul II or Benedict XVI or any pope — on abortion is much more than a personal divergence of opinion. It is to break from him in his official teaching office; in other words, it is to reject the authority of the Church itself by dissenting from one of its ancient moral doctrines.

A similar contrast, although not identical, can be drawn when speaking of capital punishment. The ancient teaching of the Church is that capital punishment can, in principle, be justified, and the many anti-death-penalty statements made by John Paul II in the last twenty years or so do not constitute a repudiation of that teaching. What the pope *did* say[51] is that the death penalty, while still acceptable as a matter of principle, is for practical purposes unwarranted in modern societies with effective criminal-justice systems. As a sign to the world of the preciousness of human life, then, criminals who could otherwise be justifiably executed should instead be imprisoned until natural death.

This papal judgment needs to be given more weight than his negative judgment (if indeed he made one) about the Iraq war, and this for three reasons. For one, he was quite explicit on many occasions over many years in his death-penalty statements, whereas his supposed condemnation of the Iraq war was ambiguous and, at most, implicit. Second, when he spoke on the death penalty, he wasn't speaking about a passing event, such as a war, but about a perennial social issue. Third, he quite explicitly said that his disapprobation of capital punishment was based on the traditional Catholic teaching of respect for human life.

Nevertheless there is room — not much room, but some room — for a Catholic to disagree with the pope on the issue of capital punishment without clashing with Church teaching. He can cite the longstanding Catholic moral tradition that the death penalty is not *ipso facto* immoral. He can further argue that he understands the realities of American society better than the pope does, and that those realities require the availability of capital punishment in *this* country or in this or that particular

[51] See, for example, the 1995 encyclical *Evangelium Vitae*.

American state. For the pope's exhortation on the death penalty depends on circumstances, but his condemnation of abortion — or rather, the Church's authoritative condemnation of abortion — does not.[52]

And so this defense of the Catholic-Democratic combination also falls to the ground. A Catholic Democrat who supports the pro-abortion cause (even if this person happens to be "personally opposed" to abortion) is directly contravening an ancient moral teaching of the Church, while a Catholic who supports the war in Iraq and even the death penalty isn't necessarily putting himself in direct opposition to the teachings of the Church.

But, of course, even if the pro-war, pro-capital punishment Catholic were just as inconsistent in his Catholicism as the pro-abortion Catholic Democrats are, this wouldn't prove that the pro-abortion Catholic Democrats are right. It would prove only that *both* were wrong.

SEPARATION OF CHURCH AND STATE: *"We don't live in a theocracy."*

At first glance, an excuse that appeals to the "separation of church and state" seems to be among the silliest rationales for a Catholic's support of the secularized Democratic Party. This separation, so we're told, is enshrined in the First Amendment to the Constitution, and it prohibits the intrusion of religion into the affairs of government. Yet the First Amendment says nothing about keeping religion out of government; it's concerned instead with

[52] I'm not saying that I myself approve of the death penalty in America, for I don't. All I'm saying is that it isn't necessarily inconsistent to be an American Catholic while at the same time favoring the death penalty.

keeping government out of religion. Its two religion "clauses"[53] say (1) that there will be no "establishment of religion" and (2) that there will be no interference with the "free exercise" of religion. That's it: government must keep its hands off religion; nothing about religion keeping its hands off government.

However, it should be considered that in writing the religion section of the First Amendment, the framers were no doubt remembering the history of England and how the government of that nation, from the time of Henry VIII until what was then the present day (the 1780s), established a national religion and interfered with the free exercise of dissenting religions. This was a case of government controlling religion, but at the same time it was a case of religion controlling government. That is to say, government persecuted, or at least discriminated against, all religions other than the Church of England, but one of the main reasons it did so was because the Church of England, both through its bishops and its lay members, had tremendous influence over government (only members of the Church of England could serve in Parliament or government). In other words, in its competition with other churches, not to mention its competition with outright infidelity, the Church of England used government to put down the church's rivals.

This is the kind of thing people, many of them Catholics, have in mind when they say that advocating laws against abortion or same-sex marriage violates the principle of separation of church and state. They fear that an alliance of conservative churches might someday gain enough governmental power to impose religious

[53] There's some dispute among scholars as to whether these should be counted as two clauses or simply as two parts of a single clause.

values on everybody else, non-believers included. This is what they mean when they speak, as they often do, of the looming danger of "theocracy." Behind the moral-conservative political activism of Christian churches they see would-be theocrats, or "dominionists," who want to take over America, stamp out abortion, subjugate women, drive homosexuals back into the closet, and enact other items allegedly on the agenda of the Religious Right. Yet this would be clearly un-American, violating the philosophical, religious, and moral pluralism that has long been, and *should* be, characteristic of the United States.

One obvious and oft-given answer is this: few liberals have made similar objections to the modern civil-rights movement, which was in large measure inspired by religion and based on churches. Martin Luther King, Jr. was a Protestant minister — even, it might be said, a Christian martyr. Are the objectors ready to say that the great legislative fruits of this religio-political movement, the Civil Rights Act of 1964 and the Voting Rights Act of 1965, are illegitimate, that they're instances of the imposition of theocratic values? Will they say that the spirit of American "pluralism" demanded that the pro-segregation values of the KKK and other racists should have been respected? Of course not. And so it appears that what's at stake for these people isn't a matter of principle (separation of church and state) but a matter of policy. Some policies they like (e.g., civil-rights legislation), and some they dislike (e.g., laws restricting abortion). A religion-driven politics is okay when it produces laws they like, but it's very naughty when it produces laws they don't like. And so we may conclude (may we not?) that all this talk about the separation of church and state is nothing but dust they throw in people's eyes.

But the separationists have a counter-rejoinder to make. It's an accidental fact, they'll say, that the civil-rights movement was so heavily cloaked in Christianity. For you didn't have to be a Christian to approve and support the movement: many Jews supported it, as did many religiously indifferent persons, as did many outright secularists. In fact, in percentage terms, secularist support for King and his movement was undoubtedly higher than was Christian support. Many Christians (especially among white Southerners) were opposed, while virtually every secularist in America approved. Equal rights for African-Americans wasn't a distinctively Christian belief — no, it was a belief that appealed to *all reasonable persons*. The more reasonable you were, the more you approved of it. The test question, then, for proposed laws or policies that are somehow entangled with religion should be this: *Are they reasonable?* Do they appeal to reasonable persons regardless of their religious beliefs or non-beliefs? Or are they the kind of laws and policies that appeal only to persons of a certain religious orientation?

Using this "reasonable person" principle, those who oppose laws that would restrict abortion argue that such laws do not appeal to all or almost all reasonable persons; instead they very narrowly appeal to certain kinds of old-fashioned religious believers — conservative Protestants, traditional Catholics, Orthodox Jews, Mormons, and so forth. And therefore such laws would be wrong — violations of the American principle of religious tolerance.

This comes close to being a very good point. If Catholics (and other conservative religious believers) had no "reasonable" basis for their proposed anti-abortion laws, if their basis were simply revelation ("this is what the Bible says" or "this is what the Church says"), then they would have no right, under the American rules of the game, to "impose" their anti-abortion values on society at large. In medieval Europe or seventeenth-century Massachusetts, they could have passed laws based on revelation alone, but not in modern America.

And so Catholics who would like to legislate against abortion (or against same-sex marriage, and so on) have to do two things. First, they have to show that opposition to abortion isn't simply a matter of faith and revelation; rather, a "reasonable" case can be made for it. Pro-life advocates have been making this case for decades now, arguing as a point of reason, not religion, that the unborn are human beings with a right to life from the moment of conception, and arguing as a point of common sense that if there's some doubt as to the humanity of the unborn, the benefit of that doubt should be given to life. We shouldn't kill something that *might be* an innocent human being until we're quite sure that it's *not* a human being. And to date nobody has been able to come close to proving this negative.

Of course, anti-abortion Catholics have to recognize the vast numbers of apparently reasonable people — secularists, liberal Christians, and others — who are unconvinced by these reasonable arguments. If the anti-abortion case is reasonable, shouldn't everybody, or at least almost everybody, be convinced by it? Reasonable arguments show that murder, rape, and robbery are wrong, and the result is that all reasonable persons believe that murder, rape, and robbery are wrong. The fact that not all reasonable people agree with the argument that abortion is wrong — doesn't this show that the anti-abortion argument isn't really reasonable?

And yet if the question, "Is slavery morally wrong?" had been asked of Americans in the 1850s, there would have been a division of opinion. People who were to all appearances reasonable would have disagreed, reasonable Northerners saying it's wrong, reasonable Southerners saying it's right. But this lack of consensus didn't prove that there was no reasonable answer to the question. There *was* a reasonable answer, and it was this: that slavery is morally wrong. But why did so many apparently reasonable Southerners fail to see that this was the answer? Because, as we can all see now, a century and a half later, on that particular question their rationality had been trumped by their self-interest (as slaveholders), by a lifetime of pro-slavery propaganda, by very strong race prejudice, or by a combination of these factors.

In a parallel way, Catholics (and their conservative Protestant allies) can account for the fact that so many apparently reasonable Americans reject what Catholics believe to be the reasonable case against abortion. This rejection is due not to a lack of rationality in the argument but to a lack of rationality in those who reject the argument. When it comes to abortion, their rationality has been trumped by a number of factors: anti-Christian prejudice, many decades of propaganda in defense of sexual liberation and abortion, and plain self-interest (the self-interest of those who have obtained or might obtain an abortion, of those who are employed by abortion clinics, and of those who have a financial investment in the abortion industry). Yet as long as Catholics make their case against abortion on rational or "reasonable" grounds, not simply by appealing to revelation, they're playing by the American rules of the game, and so they can't be accused of violating even the *spirit* of "separation of church and state." Provided they do that, those who accuse them of aiming at the creation of a theocracy are talking nonsense.

There are, of course, probably as many excuses for remaining a Catholic Democrat as there are Catholic Democrats. But these are by and large the most popular, and the ones on which many other excuses are based. Particular ones may pass in and out of fashion, but as long as being both Catholic and Democratic creates cognitive dissonance — that is, as long as the Democratic Party stands with the enemies of Christianity — I doubt we shall ever see the end of them.

Chapter 6

The Political Future of Catholics and the Democratic Party

Over the last twenty or thirty years, an immense amount of damage has been done to the Democratic Party by its alliance with moral liberalism on Culture War issues. If the United States were made up of New York, New England, California, Seattle, Ann Arbor, Madison, and a few other places of like mind, being four-square in favor of abortion rights and same-sex marriage would be a politically smart position to take. Unfortunately for the party, the United States also contains such inconvenient and "backward" places as South Carolina, Alabama, Texas, and South Dakota.

The ideal solution for the Democrats would be to expel the secularists from the party, thereby forcing them, if they wished to remain politically active, to create a third party made up of the liberal ultra-left. But, as I said earlier, secularists are now too powerful a force within the party to be expelled. Indeed, to call for the expulsion of secularists is, in effect, to ask them to expel themselves, so strong is their position of power. They wouldn't abdicate their power over the party even if they deemed that it would thereby win more elections, for what use to them would be victories by a Democratic Party that had divorced itself from secularism and the values of moral liberalism? No, even if they were convinced that they and their values have caused the Democrats to slide downhill in recent decades, they'd say, "So what? We might be losing now, but the tide of cultural history is running in our favor; we'll just hold on to our dominant position in one of America's great political parties until our day finally arrives, and then we'll win victory after victory."

But the party could entertain less drastic remedies, remedies that secularists might conceivably endorse. The most obvious of these is to allow, even to encourage, the United States Supreme Court to overturn its 1973 *Roe v. Wade* decision, the ruling that declared abortion to be a constitutionally protected right. This would not, as much liberal propaganda suggests (in a deliberately dishonest way), make abortion illegal. It would simply mean that abortion wouldn't be constitutionally protected, and that the decision as to how much abortion, if any, should be allowed would be made by the legislatures of the fifty states. In all likelihood, the liberal ("blue") states would enact highly permissive abortion laws while the conservative ("red") states would enact laws restricting abortion in various degrees. When the dust cleared, state abortion laws would probably run the full spectrum from abortion-on-demand at one end to no-abortion at the other, with every imaginable intermediate instance between the two extremes.

From the secularist point of view, of course, this would not be an ideal situation, but it would be a bearable one. Abortion would still be legal in America, and widely available. For those women in highly restrictive states, getting an abortion would be no easy thing, requiring in some cases a long and expensive trip out of state. But if moral liberals are the great believers in abortion that they claim to be (and there's no reason to believe that they're not), and if they're on average fairly affluent (which they are), then they could fund scholarships (they could be called "abortionships") to transport low-income girls and women from, say, Alabama or Mississippi to some blue state for an abortion, putting them up at a motel for a night or two. If those in the pro-abortion community were willing to put their money where their mouths are, then even in a post-*Roe* era, very few American women who wanted to have abortions would be unable to have them.

As a pro-life person myself, I would, of course, be unhappy to see such an arrangement prevail. But that it *could* prevail proves that the pro-choice element in the Democratic Party (an element that includes virtually every important Democrat in America) can give up its defense of *Roe v. Wade* while effectively protecting its "value" of abortion.

If *Roe* were overturned, the great American abortion struggle wouldn't disappear, but its ferocity would diminish. It would continue to be fought in state legislatures, but no longer on the national level — or, if it went on there, it would do so in a much diminished way. Abortion would no longer be a big issue in presidential or congressional elections. Future appointments to the Supreme Court would no longer hinge on how the nominee feels about abortion. The battles at the state capitols, if you added them all together, would very probably not equal the current ferocity of today's national abortion struggle. That's because in Washington and at the national level, the two sides are pretty evenly matched; as a result, both sides are motivated to try just a little harder, to fight just a little more ferociously, trying to tip the balance. In most states, by contrast, one side or the other will clearly have the upper hand, and in most of those places, the weaker party will lack the resources and the will to fight fiercely.

Getting the abortion fight off the national stage would make it possible for the Democrats once again to win control of Congress and the White House. Working-class and lower-middle-class voters who would be "natural" Democrats if elections were to hinge mainly on economic issues would once again feel at ease voting Democratic. It's a grave misfortune both for the party and for the nation that the party has largely fallen into the control of secularists who prefer ideological purity to winning elections. Every time the party loses an election because of its Culture War alliance with the secularist side, it loses an opportunity to enact programs that would benefit "natural" Democrats. But as long as the party remains "pure" on issues such as abortion, these ideologues won't be much bothered that the economic interests of working-class and middle-class families get neglected.

The political future of American Catholics

Given the anti-Christian nature of today's Democratic Party, it's easy to see why Catholics are abandoning the party, and it's hard to see why even more Catholics won't abandon it as years go by. As it gradually sinks into the minds of serious Catholics that the Democratic Party is an anti-Christian party, even more Catholics will leave their old Democratic home and move in with the Republicans.

But will it sink in? Yes, I think it will, and this for three reasons. First, there's the fact itself. The more deeply the party becomes enmeshed with the secularist agenda, the more evident this fact will become and the harder it will be to keep it a secret. Second, increasingly there will be those who recognize it and sound the alarm — this book being one such example. Third, the weak and ineffective episcopal leadership that has plagued the American Church for decades might not last forever. When and if a stronger cohort of bishops arrives on the scene, Catholics will be more frequently reminded that their religion is under attack and see that the Democratic Party has allied itself with the attackers. (We see such effective leadership at work already among evangelical Protestants, who tend to have a greater awareness of the issues and stakes surrounding the Culture War.)

The Catholic population of the United States (by which I mean, in this case, all those people who *call* themselves Catholic) is divided into three main groups: one, the more or less orthodox Catholics; another, those who are liberal Catholics; and third, those who haven't taken the trouble to decide whether they're orthodox or liberal — they're "wait and see" Catholics.

Unless either the Democrats or the Republicans drastically change their stripes, it seems to me very likely that almost all the first group (the orthodox) will eventually end up in Republican ranks as that party increasingly reinforces its image as the pro-Christian party; and that many, although by no means all, of the second group (the liberals) will stay with the Democrats as that party increasingly reinforces its image as the party opposed to traditional Christianity. The third group ("wait and see" Catholics) will mostly drift toward the Republican Party, for even though they have no strong adhesion to orthodoxy, they'll prefer a Republican Party that defends Christianity to a Democratic Party that attacks it.

Once upon a time it was the most natural thing in the world for a Catholic to be a Democrat. In the foreseeable future, unless the Democrats drastically change their present anti-Christian course, it will be the most natural thing in the world for a Catholic to be a Republican.

Postscript

My Own Political Future

Since I'm now in my late sixties, my days as an active politician are pretty much over. But I continue to *support* active politicians — with my advice, my volunteering in their campaigns, and my money contributions. But which party will I support? To judge from what I've said in the entire course of this book, you'd think that I, a Catholic of the orthodox type, would support the Republican Party. That might be the general rule for people of my type; but, as often happens, the general rule doesn't apply to the particular case. I remain a Democrat. My voter registration card at the Newport City Hall shows that I'm a Democrat. You can look it up.

My participation in politics is a local thing ("All politics is local," as Tip O'Neill famously said), and in my state, Rhode Island, there isn't much difference between Democrats and Republicans when it comes to an issue like abortion. In both parties there are people on the pro-Christian and anti-Christian side. For instance, the Republican U.S. senator from Rhode Island, Lincoln Chafee, has a solidly pro-choice voting record in Washington. But so has our Democratic senator, Jack Reed (an old colleague and ally of mine from the Rhode Island Senate). A small state, Rhode Island has only two members of the U.S. House, both Democrats. One of them, Patrick Kennedy, votes pro-choice (except on partial-birth abortion); the other, Jim Langevin, votes pro-life. The state legislature contains both pro-lifers and pro-choicers, and the division between the two isn't along party lines. So why should I abandon a state Democratic Party that has a notable number of pro-choicers in order that I may team up with a Republican Party that has just as many? If I have to be connected with one radically imperfect party or the other, why not stick with the party that has lots of my old friends and colleagues in it?

Somebody might say that, given the mixed nature of the two parties, I should abstain from all political involvement whatsoever: a plague on both their houses. But I'd regard that as poor citizenship on my part. In a democratic republic, the most fundamental of all citizenship duties, it seems to me, is to vote in elections; and not far behind that is the duty to help worthwhile political candidates.

My general attitude is to approach elections with a presumption in favor of Democratic candidates: especially when they're pro-life, or there's no pro-life opponent, or when the candidate is an old friend. But it's a rebuttable presumption. If there's something wrong with the Democratic candidate — often this has to do with abortion, but it might also be that he's a fool or a knave — then I cast the presumption aside.

Sometimes I *vote* for Republican candidates. That happens only when the Democrat is pro-choice and the Republican is either pro-life or less clearly pro-choice than the Democrat. But although I sometimes vote for Republicans, I never volunteer for their campaigns or make financial contributions to them.[54] In

[54] There has been only one exception to this rule. The son of one of my fellow professors once ran for Congress as a

sum, I'm still a Democrat, but no longer the "yellow dog" Democrat I was once upon a time.

One of the reasons I remain with the party is that it's an old habit, so old that it's now part of my personal identity. Although I didn't become a registered Democrat until the age of twenty-one, I've had the feeling of being a Democrat since before I was ten years old, since the time when my father told me that "we" are Democrats because the Democratic Party is the party of "poor people" like ourselves. I'm now sixty-eight years old — too late in life to go in search of a new political identity.

Another reason is that I was a Democrat before the secularists seized control of the party; I was a Democrat in the days when being a Democrat had nothing to do with endorsing abortion or same-sex marriage or with undermining the Christian religion. No matter how unpleasant I might find their company, I refuse to let the secularists and moral liberals evict me from a house I occupied before they did.

Still another reason is that I feel I can make a more valuable contribution to the conservative side in the Culture War from *inside* the party than from outside. It's easy to ignore criticisms of secularism and moral liberalism coming from Republicans; such criticisms can be chalked up to partisan motives. It's somewhat less easy to ignore criticisms coming from an old Democrat with good Democratic credentials. I want to do what I can to preserve the honor of the Democratic Party. I believe the day will eventually come (long after I'm in the grave, I fear) when the party, if it survives, will look back on its anti-Christian decades with shame and embarrassment — just as it now looks back on its pro-slavery

pro-life Republican from western Massachusetts. I looked the other way and wrote him a check for a small amount.

and soft-on-segregation days with shame and embarrassment. When that day arrives, it will be consoling for some people to remember that not all Democrats endorsed this turn to the anti-Christian left.

But for me it isn't just a matter of old attachments to the Democratic Party. It's also a matter of being repelled by the Republican Party. This is an old prejudice, I suppose, stemming from my childhood political socialization. I've always thought of the Republican Party — and I still think of it — as "the party of the rich." Now, there's nothing wrong with being rich (I wish I were rich myself). Nor do I think there's anything wrong with the rich controlling a major political party; that seems to me quite normal, and politically healthy. But this just happens not to be the kind of political party I want to belong to.

This unwillingness to belong to the party of the rich might stem from my Catholic education — an education that held up for admiration the life of voluntary poverty led by Jesus Christ and by centuries of Christian monks and nuns. Or it might be that, after having spent my childhood living in a working-class environment and my adult life living in a lower-middle-class environment, I don't consider affluent people to be "my" people. Or it might be that when I was a member of the Rhode Island Senate I represented a mostly non-affluent constituency. Or it might simply be envy: I'd like to be rich, but I'm not. Whatever the reason, I'd much prefer to belong to a party that represents the interests and concerns — including the moral concerns — of the "little people."

Can I imagine any set of circumstances under which I might totally abandon the Democratic Party and turn Republican? Yes, two sets of circumstances. In one, it turns out that one of those emails I keep getting from Nigeria proves to be valid and $50 million is deposited in my bank account. I'd then say, "Screw the little people" and become an enthusiastic Republican demanding tax cuts. In the other, the Republican Party becomes the party of the little people. That this might happen isn't totally inconceivable. The exodus of the little people from the Democratic Party into the Republican Party has been going on for more than three decades now. White conservative Protestants are now solidly Republican. Orthodox Catholics will soon be solidly Republican. Other groups might follow — including African-Americans, almost all of whom are religiously conservative. If enough of the little people end up in the Republican Party, the structure of the party will change.

I doubt that such a development, if it ever takes place, will take place during my lifetime; but if it does, I'll become a Republican. In the meantime I'll remain a cranky and complaining Democrat.

Appendices

Appendix I

An Expanded Definition of Secularism

Since my subject throughout much of this book is secularism, I ought to define in more detail what I mean when I use the word. In the course of the last three hundred years, there have been many varieties of secularism in the Western world (Appendix II traces their development). Here, however, I'm concerned only with contemporary American secularism, which, as I'm using the term, has three essential characteristics.

- *Atheism.* Secularists are either atheists or agnostics; at all events, they're religious unbelievers. If atheists, they're ontological or metaphysical naturalists; that is to say, they hold that nature (the universe) is all there is: there's no God; there's no supernatural realm. If agnostics, they're epistemological or methodological naturalists, holding that even if there is a realm of being beyond nature (the Unknowable of the nineteenth-century English agnostic philosopher Herbert Spencer), we humans are incapable of knowing anything about it. Hence, for all practical purposes, it makes sense to live our lives as though this hypothetical supernatural realm (including God) did not exist.

Abstractly speaking, it's possible for an agnostic to tilt either toward atheism or toward religious belief. The French philosopher-scientist-mathematician Blaise Pascal (1623-1662) is an outstanding example of a philosophical agnostic who moved all the way to the religious-belief end of the spectrum. In the case of American secularist agnostics, however, the movement is very strong in the opposite direction. They're strongly inclined toward atheism; it's just that they're temperamentally more cautious in their assertions than are the outright atheists, more unwilling to offend the sensitivities of their religion-believing neighbors, and reluctant to close the door absolutely on the exceedingly thin and remote possibility of the supernatural. But practically speaking, there's barely a dime's worth of difference between secularist atheists and secularist agnostics.

• *Anti-Christianity.* Secularists are hostile toward religion in general and toward Christianity in particular. They regard Christianity as both intellectually foolish and morally wicked. Their special hostility toward Christianity, however, isn't based on a belief that Christianity is worse than other major religions; all of them are seen by secularists as bad. But Christianity just happens to be the dominant religion in Western history generally and American history in particular; even today it's the dominant religion in America, a very powerful force. And so, to secularists, who feel called to fight against the evils of religion, Christianity is the obvious and most important enemy.

Secularists considerably tone down their opposition to religion, however, when it comes to certain special cases. Many make something of an exception for Buddhism, which they regard as having considerable merit. But the Buddhism they have in mind isn't Buddhism as actually practiced by ordinary people in East

Asia. Rather, they have in mind Buddhism as it originally came from the hands of Gautama himself, or more exactly, what they have in mind is original Buddhism as represented by present-day Western proponents of Buddhism. And this kind of Buddhism is more a philosophy than a religion; indeed, it's a philosophy one of whose aims is to undermine popular religion. It's represented as a non-theistic or atheistic religion — just the kind of "religion" that might prove popular with the kind of people who are on the lookout for "spirituality" but don't like religion or belief in God.

Another special case is Islam. It isn't that secularists approve of Islam in any way. Far from it. But at times they have a certain sneaking sympathy for Islam on the principle of "the enemy of my enemy is my friend." For many centuries large sections of the Muslim world have felt intense hostility toward Christianity; and since the events of 9/11, many Christians of a more or less fundamentalist stripe have reciprocated this sentiment (thereby reviving the anti-Islamic sentiments of medieval Europe). In this Christian-versus-Muslim struggle, many secularists at times give a quiet little cheer for the Muslims.

Yet another special case is Christianity as found among African-Americans. In general, secularists are strongly sympathetic toward American blacks, this strong sympathy being one of the great claims to moral superiority made by secularists; as they see it, they, in a racist society, are outstandingly pure in their rejection of racism. If you're sympathetic to blacks, you have no choice but to be sympathetic to their culture (no matter how little it is to your personal taste), and an important part of their culture is Christianity and the black churches and the music of the black churches. So when you attack Christianity, you must keep your fire focused on the religion as practiced by white people, averting your eyes as far as possible from the Christianity of African-Americans.

And still another special case is Orthodox Judaism. In principle you're free to denounce this religion, but few do. For although its beliefs and moral code are as objectionable as those of Christianity, perhaps even more so, it's small potatoes when compared with that giant thing, Christianity. So why waste time attacking it? For another thing, although Jews of this classical kind are different from Conservative Jews and Reform Jews and very different indeed from the many Jews who are thoroughly nonreligious, still there's a kind of solidarity that subsists among Jews of all persuasions, from the Orthodox at one end of the spectrum to outright atheists at the other. And so an attack on Orthodox Jews might be felt by other Jews as an attack on *all* Jews; in other words, there's a real danger that it will be perceived as a kind of anti-Semitism. But a secularist will no more want to be accused of anti-Semitism than of racism. Hence, secularist attacks on religion, although they implicitly condemn Orthodox Judaism, almost never do so explicitly. Besides, Orthodox Judaism has from of old (and not entirely without reason) been suspicious of and hostile toward Christianity. From the secularist point of view, the erstwhile enemy of my enemy should be treated as my honorary friend.

The most important exception to secularists' anti-religion hostility is what's usually called "liberal Christianity." The kind of Christianity really detested by secularism is the kind of Christianity that may be called classical or old-fashioned or traditional or orthodox: the kind found among orthodox Catholics, conservative Protestants, and traditional Eastern Orthodox believers. This is the variety of Christianity that adheres to the beliefs of the ancient creeds (e.g., the creeds of Nicea and Chalcedon),[55] that

[55] Many conservative Protestants don't accept the authority of the creeds, since they accept the Bible as the sole

accepts the Bible as authoritative, and that, in the name of old-fashioned Christian morality, rejects the modern sexual revolution and holds, for example, that abortion and homosexuality are sinful.

From the secularist point of view, liberal Christians aren't nearly so bad. Indeed they seem ready to meet secularism halfway: they no longer swallow the ancient creeds whole; they generally don't believe in such "irrational" articles as the Trinity, the divinity of Christ, the Virgin Birth, and the Resurrection. They read the Bible quite freely and rationally, not with superstition or anything approaching slavish literalism. And while they have certain reservations about the modern sexual revolution, they've abandoned the sexual absolutism that's typical of old-time Christianity; they can, in very many cases, if not in all, accept abortion and same-sex marriage as morally legitimate. While secularists don't precisely approve of liberal Christianity (for despite its merits, it still has too much Christianity about it and too little liberalism), nonetheless it's the kind of thing they can cooperate with in many areas. Once again, the enemy of my enemy is my friend.

- *Moral liberalism*. The message of secularism isn't merely negative. When it comes to morality, secularists have a positive message, a new and (as they see it) better morality that they recommend to the world — as opposed to the old Christian morality. This morality may be called, and usually is called, "moral liberalism."

authority, the sole rule of faith. At the same time, however, their interpretation of the Bible is such that they end up agreeing with the articles of the creeds. And thus they agree with the creeds without accepting them as authoritative.

A secularist can stand on one leg while reciting the two great principles of moral liberalism:

- The Personal Liberty Principle (PLP), according to which a person is morally free to do whatever he or she wishes, provided only that the person so acting does nothing to hurt others.

- The Tolerance Principle (TP), according to which we must tolerate the conduct of others, provided this conduct doesn't hurt someone else.

The PLP and the TP are obviously two sides of the same coin: if action X is permitted by the PLP, it must be tolerated by the TP; we mustn't interfere with any morally permissible conduct.[56]

According to the traditional Christian idea, immorality is better named "sin," and sin can be defined as an offense against God. But for the secularist, who believes himself to be living in a world without God, the only person whom I might offend by this or that conduct is another human being. And so this becomes the nature of immorality: not an infringement on the rights of God, but an infringement on the rights of another human being. Conduct that hurts only myself might be stupid — might even be so stupid that

[56] In fairness to moral liberals, there's more to their moral theory than the PLP and the TP. They also have what may be called a morality of aspiration: whether out of manufactured humanist principles, or based on vestigial traces of Christian formation, they admire and recommend acts of kindness and of love, or at least deeds that they consider to be acts of kindness and of love. Thus, they admire persons who dedicate their lives, or a portion of their lives, to protecting the environment, to serving the poor, to defending the rights of women and homosexuals, and so forth.

it's tragic — but by definition it can't be immoral. Likewise, an action isn't immoral if the person who gets hurt was a consenting adult participant. To take a somewhat exotic example: If Mr. A and Ms. B, both consenting adults, are engaged in a sadomasochistic relationship, and if B inflicts physical pain on A, there's no immorality involved, since A waived his right not to be caused pain.

Secularists are rarely clear as to precisely what they mean by "harm to others." Sometimes they mean something very simple and obvious: I pull out a gun and shoot a clerk at a liquor store. Without question, this is immoral, for it involves hurt to another person that is direct, tangible, obvious, and immediate. But sometimes they mean something more complex and sophisticated, a hurt that is indirect, mediate, relatively intangible, far from obvious. Many environmental concerns held by secularists are like this.[57] It's wrong to drive an SUV because SUVs use a lot of gas and contribute to the greenhouse effect; this in turn raises the temperature of the earth, causing strange weather patterns (which have perhaps resulted in the destruction of New Orleans), melting polar ice caps, and giving people skin cancer. Similarly moral liberals consider it immoral to expose innocent bystanders to secondhand cigarette smoke, even though the harm it might cause, if any, will be minor and likely undetectable until many years later, if ever.

Oddly, when it comes to matters related to sexual conduct, moral liberals usually revert to a simplistic standard of direct, tangible, obvious, and immediate harm. Thus, there must be no moral

[57] While not all environmentalists are secularists, most secularists are environmentalists. Protecting the environment is one of their principal moral concerns.

restriction (and certainly no legal restriction) on sexual conduct among consenting adults. In what way do two people directly hurt anyone by engaging in sexual conduct? Of course, as an indirect result of moral liberalism's project of eroding traditional sexual norms, our nation now has tremendously high divorce and out-of-wedlock birthrates, tens of millions of kids who have grown up without fathers, women who can't escape poverty because of their status as unmarried mothers, high rates of sexually transmitted diseases, a gigantic pornography industry, an epidemic of sexual crimes, and more than one million abortions per year. Yet somehow moral liberals, so sensitive to the wickedness of driving an SUV, can't see any wickedness in rampant sexual license. Clearly their application of the "harm to others" principle depends on the subject matter to which the principle is being applied, and the subject of sex is afforded a great deal of tolerance.

What lies behind this inconsistency, I submit, is this: moral liberalism isn't mainly a matter of principle, neither the PLP nor the TP. Rather, it's foremost a means of eliminating traditional Christian morality, and it deems that the PLP and the TP, whatever their shortcomings as ethical principles, can be successfully deployed to that end. The PLP and TP aren't so much ethical principles as they are items of effective propaganda.

At the time it emerged in the Mediterranean basin, Christianity rigorously banned a series of practices that the prevailing morality of the Greco-Roman world condoned: non-marital sex, easy divorce, homosexuality, abortion, infanticide, and suicide. From the time of the social triumph of Christianity in the fourth century until just the other day, these practices were generally condemned by the culture of the Western world. The program of moral liberalism, which has been successful at winning vast numbers of converts in recent decades, not just in the United States but perhaps even more in Europe, involves a re-legitimization of the practices banned by Christianity. Greeks and Romans of the age of Augustus would feel at home if they were able to return to the world of the late twentieth and early twenty-first centuries.

I don't mean to say, as conservative critics of modernity often do, that our world is once again turning "pagan." Possibly it is, but my point is that moral liberalism, whether it eventually takes us in the direction of neopaganism or not, is out to supplant the distinctive morality of Christianity with a morality that legitimizes abortion, euthanasia, and most kinds of sexual liberty. If Christianity had traditionally condemned driving SUVs, secularists would be ardent champions of SUV ownership.

Appendix II

The History of American Secularism

Secularism, of course, didn't fall from the sky just the other day. Nor did it spring full-grown from the collective forehead of the ACLU or NARAL. It has a long history of development in America.

In the last few centuries there have been many varieties of secularism, all sharing a basic anti-Christianity combined with an attempt to replace the traditional, transcendent Christian worldview with an alternative, this-worldly philosophy. Leaving aside isolated individuals in the medieval and early modern period, secularism began to be a significant cultural force with the "freethinkers" of the late-seventeenth and early-eighteenth centuries — in particular, English Deists such as John Toland, Matthew Tindal, and Anthony Collins. Deistic secularism soon jumped to France (which henceforth became the heartland of the movement), where its leading figure was Voltaire, the most popular and influential writer of the eighteenth century. Before the century ended, Deism would spread to Germany, Italy, Scotland, and the United States.

These Deists shared five fundamental doctrines:

1. God can be known by reason, and by reason alone: the order of the universe is sufficient evidence for the existence of God without the need for revelation.

2. This God (or Nature, God's creation) has provided us with a natural — again, as opposed to revealed — knowledge of the fundamental principles of morality: either we know them innately or we can figure them out by reason. This explains why the fundamental rules of morality are much the same in every age and all over the world.

3. There are no such things as miracles. Why would an all-knowing and all-powerful Creator have to "correct" his creation from time to time? Wouldn't he have gotten it right the first time?

4. There has never been a special revelation from God to humans — neither to Jews nor to Christians nor to Muslims nor to anybody else. The "holy books" of these religions are nothing more than manmade creations.

5. These so-called revealed religions, insofar as they go beyond the teachings of Deism, are false and often pernicious, the products of fraud or delusion or both. Mankind will be better off when these false religions disappear and are replaced by Deism.

All Deism was anti-Christian, but this anti-Christianity came in "hard" and "soft" varieties. The typical "hard" anti-Christian was Voltaire.[58] He detested the religion, and through his writings — many of them satirical, others filled with indignation — he

[58] François-Marie Arouet (1694-1778).

made aggressive moral and intellectual war against it. The motto of his later years was "Crush the infamous thing" (*"Ecrasez l'infâme"*). A typical "soft" anti-Christian was the German philosopher Immanuel Kant, who, without exhibiting any strong animosity toward Christianity (the religion of his youth), attempted to show the weakness of Christianity and the religious superiority of Deism in his very deistically titled book, *Religion Within the Limits of Reason Alone* (first published in 1793).

In nineteenth-century Europe, following that gigantic watershed event, the French Revolution, there emerged three main currents of secularism. For one, there was the "liberal" and anti-clerical current, found in many countries, especially Catholic countries — but above all in France, where anti-clericals were the chief founders of the Third Republic. Some of these anti-clericals, faithful to Voltaire, were Deists; but by the second half of the century, many of the most prominent among them were agnostics or atheists. Their great practical goals included a strong separation of church and state and a national education system that would be totally nonreligious in management and curricular content.

There was also the socialist-communist current, which was explicitly atheistic. At a minimum, it hoped to drive religion from the public sphere and reduce it to no more than a private practice. At a maximum, it hoped to eradicate religion from the cultural life of society by means of persecution and atheistic propaganda.

Then there was the nationalistic current (which in France often tended to merge with the anti-clericalism). As a rule nationalism was not explicitly anti-Christian, and in fact, it often claimed to have a Christian character. But it was de facto anti-Christian, in that it considered the nation to be both more important than the Church and more worthy of devotion than God. God and Christianity were valued only to the degree that they endorsed the nation and gave it their support — no more. In the event of a conflict arising between the nation and Christianity, it was the latter that would have to give way — for example, in Bismarck's *Kulturkampf* between the new German Reich and the Catholic Church.

In the twentieth century the socialist-communist current triumphed in Soviet Russia and many other eastern- or central-European countries, leading to a severe persecution of Christianity. The nationalist current too had far-reaching effects, leading first to World War I, then to Nazism in Germany and the Second World War. In the aftermath of the horrors of the two world wars, nationalism — at least the kind that trumped God and the Church — went into decline in Europe, thereby opening the road to the creation of the transnational European Union. The Soviet Union having been on the winning side in World War II, Communism had a longer life than nationalism; but the absurdity of Communism as a social and economic system finally caused it to collapse in Europe by the end of the century.

By then Europe was free of Communism and almost entirely free (except for a few skinheads here and there) of the strong varieties of nationalism, and today the only form of secularism thriving in Europe is a form that's a lineal successor of nineteenth-century liberal anti-clericalism. There's almost no Deism left; today's secularists are either atheists or agnostics. And they're also highly individualistic, a far cry from the anti-individualistic type of secularist who, a few generations ago, were recruited into the Communist or Nazi parties; a far cry too from the kind of non-individualists who have been typical members of the Catholic Church. These modern European secularists pride themselves on their tolerance and open-mindedness, especially their sexual open-mindedness.

Secularism in America: Deists

Although present from the beginning of the Republic, secularism in the United States has had a history far less turbulent and catastrophic than secularism in Europe. In the eighteenth century, American secularism too was deistic, and just as in Europe, there were two varieties of deistic anti-Christianity: the "hard" and the "soft" (the latter being the more common variety).

A typical "soft" Deist was Benjamin Franklin. Although as an adult he no longer went to church on Sundays, and although he regarded Deism as philosophically and religiously superior to the Christianity of his youth, Franklin nonetheless gave generous financial support to all the churches in Philadelphia. His idea was this: although Deism was superior to Christianity, still it was better for people to be Christian believers than not to be believers at all.[59]

Another famous "soft" Deist was Thomas Jefferson. He had no use for traditional Christianity, but he made no public assault on it; his criticisms were made only in private correspondence to friends. And although he rejected the idea of the divinity of Christ, he retained great admiration for the man Jesus. In this admiration, Jefferson even went so far as to produce a merged and redacted version of the four Gospels, omitting what he considered to be their false and superstitious elements, thereby leaving us with what he saw as an accurate account of the life and teachings of Jesus.[60]

[59] See Franklin's 1790 letter to Rev. Ezra Stiles, which can be found, among many other places, in Isaac Kramnick, ed., *The Portable Enlightenment Reader* (New York: Penguin Books, 1995), 166-167.

[60] See Thomas Jefferson, *The Jefferson Bible: The Life and Morals of Jesus of Nazareth* (Boston: Beacon Press, 1989).

The most famous of the American "hard" Deists was Tom Paine,[61] whose virulent anti-Christianity was expressed in his *The Age of Reason*. Rather less famous as a strong anti-Christian Deist was yet another Revolutionary War patriot, Ethan Allen, the leader of the "Green Mountain Boys," who, aided by Benedict Arnold, captured Fort Ticonderoga; he authored a big, rambling anti-Christian book with the typically deistic title of *Reason, the Only Oracle of God*.

Secularism in America: skeptics

In nineteenth-century America, unlike in Europe, there was hardly any socialism or communism. There was a great deal of nationalism, to be sure, but American nationalism never went as far as European nationalism, especially in France and Germany, in making itself a substitute for Christianity or the nation a substitute for God. The relative weakness of Christianity in Europe, where anti-clericalism and modernist ideas had taken a great toll, created a personal vacuum that nationalism was able to fill; but in America, Christianity (mostly Protestantism) remained a vibrant religion among the populace at large. The difference between the Old World and the New can be explained, at least in large measure, by the fact that while Europe was experiencing the great anti-Christian upheaval of the French Revolution and its

See as well Jefferson's 1803 letter to Benjamin Rush, which may also be found in Kramnick, pp. 163-166.

[61] That is, if Paine — who was born and grew up in England and came to America only as an adult, went back to England after the Revolutionary War, went to France to assist with the Revolution in that country, became a French citizen, spent time in prison during the Reign of Terror, and eventually returned to the United States, where he died — can be called an American at all.

Napoleonic aftermath in the late 1700s and early 1800s, the United States was experiencing at almost the same time an upheaval of an opposite nature: the so-called Second Great Awakening, a great religious revival that impacted much of the nation in the first third of the nineteenth century.

Deism and secularism were unable to flourish in this religiously saturated cultural atmosphere. But secularism, although in abeyance in early-nineteenth-century America, re-appeared after the Civil War. Two great developments in the world of science and scholarship gave powerful ammunition to the anti-Christian forces of this second stage of secularism (counting Deism as the first stage). One was the Darwinian theory of biological evolution, which undermined both confidence that God had created the world and the belief that there's a vast ontological gap separating humans from the lower animals.[62] The other was the so-called "higher criticism" of the Bible that had emerged in Germany during the course of the century, raising serious doubts in the minds of many as to the divine authorship and, indeed, the very reliability of Sacred Scripture.

So post–Civil War American secularists weren't Deists, but either skeptics (or agnostics — a new word in those days) or outright atheists. The best known of these new secularists was Clarence Darrow (1857-1938), the great defense attorney who won undying fame in the 1925 Scopes "Monkey Trial."[63] The new skeptics (and there were many besides Darrow) availed themselves of Darwinism and modern biblical criticism to attack and ridicule

[62] Darwin's *The Origin of Species* was published in 1859, and his *The Descent of Man* was published in 1871.

[63] See Darrow's amusing and very irreverent autobiography, *The Story of My Life* (DaCapo, 1996).

religion in general and Christianity in particular. Theirs was a purely negative kind of secularism: they provided no constructive alternative to religion, but simply assumed that if religion were to collapse, men and women would manage to lead better and happier lives.

Secularism in America: builders of Utopia

The third stage of American secularism was exemplified by the philosopher John Dewey (1859-1952) and his followers. Dewey gave little attention to the demolition of Christianity; he took it for granted that that project had been sufficiently carried out by others. His task was to contribute to the construction of the new social and cultural world that would replace the rapidly vanishing world of Christianity. For more than a half-century, he wrote book after book on a wide range of philosophical and non-philosophical disciplines: logic, epistemology, metaphysics, ethics, aesthetics, politics, psychology, sociology, even religion. And above all, education: for he believed that it was chiefly through the public schools that we would create a new world to replace the lost culture of Christianity. In all his many writings, Dewey offered almost no explicit criticism of Christianity; the great majority of his more casual readers might well be unaware that the *de facto* aim of his writings was to drive Christianity from the marketplace of ideas by offering a better article.

This kind of secularism might be called "progressive secularism," in the sense that it appeared during the great age of social reform that flourished for about fifteen years at the beginning of the twentieth century (this was the "progressive era" proper) and then, following a dormant period in the 1920s, reached its great climax during the administration of Franklin Roosevelt. In its full extent, this was the age that commenced with the coming of

Theodore Roosevelt and came to an end with the departure of Harry Truman from the White House. (An interesting coincidence: Truman's last year in office, 1952, was also the year of Dewey's death at the age of 92.) In saying this, I don't mean that the majority, or even a large minority, of New Deal–type politicians and political thinkers were secularists. Far from it. They, like FDR himself, were conventional religious believers, many of them Catholic. But they, like the Deweyite secularists, tended to share Dewey's optimistic belief in the virtues of social engineering; they believed, in other words, that the solutions to society's many problems were to be found not so much in Christianity as in the intelligent application of the findings of the social sciences.[64]

Secularism in America: cultural revolutionaries

If the third stage of secularism was only tacitly — even secretly — anti-Christian, the fourth and latest stage has made no secret of its contempt for Christianity. Present-day secularism emerged in the Cultural/Sexual Revolution of the 1960s and '70s. This revolution proclaimed, and is still proclaiming to this day, a sexual ethic that's thoroughly incompatible with the traditional Christian sexual ethic. The new ethic is one of great sexual freedom, giving outright approval to a host of behaviors formerly taboo and showing a lighthearted tolerance for others: premarital sex, unmarried cohabitation, homosexuality, and pornography. This new

[64] Reinhold Niebuhr and his fans were notable exceptions to this rule. Niebuhr, although very much a New Deal kind of progressive in many ways, rejected what he regarded as the naive optimism of the social scientists, and he brought Christianity into his political thinking, at least the classical Christian doctrine of Original Sin. See his *Moral Man and Immoral Society* (Charles Scribner's Sons, 1932).

ethic even tends to be tolerant of promiscuity and adultery, without quite being willing to give these things its unqualified stamp of approval; if it regards them as "sins" at all, they're only venial sins.[65]

Of course, moral liberalism isn't limited to sex; it also involves such things as abortion and euthanasia (if we count, as I do, physician-assisted suicide as a species of euthanasia). But a permissive sexual ethic is the indispensable first step to justifying these less-attractive tenets of moral liberalism. For once you can get people to throw traditional Christian sexual morality overboard, you can readily sell them on the Personal Liberty Principle and the Tolerance Principle[66] as justifications for their conduct. And once you get them to accept the PLP and the TP, by a series of simple logical steps you can get them to accept abortion (having first presumed, as abortion proponents almost always do, that the fetus is not a human being) and euthanasia. Just like that, you've substituted wholesale the secularist ethic for the Christian one — in a

[65] This explains why proponents of this new ethic have no objection (apart from certain considerations of health) to the promiscuity characteristic of the gay male subculture. It also explains why they pooh-poohed Bill Clinton's affair with Monica Lewinsky. It might have been "inappropriate," and it might have been of some concern to Hillary, but really it was no big deal — just a sexual relationship, possibly a bit naughty, between two consenting adults. President Clinton himself, a genius at understanding what his audiences wanted to hear and at appearing to be all things to all men, would speak of the Lewinsky affair (that is, after he had given up denying that the affair had ever taken place) as "sinful" when speaking to Christian audiences, but when addressing the general public (which includes many believers in sexual freedom) he'd speak of the affair as "inappropriate."

[66] See Appendix I.

way that's far easier, simpler, and more pleasurable than getting them to read the collected works of John Dewey.

In discussing the three earlier stages of American secularism (Deism, skepticism, and Dewey-ism), I was able to offer iconic individuals who typified these stages: Tom Paine and Benjamin Franklin, Clarence Darrow, and John Dewey himself. I'd like to do the same for the fourth stage, but I can't. Why not? Two reasons.

For one, this latest stage has been a *behavioral* rejection of traditional Christianity, not, as were the earlier forms of secularism, a *theory-based* rejection. Theories require theorists, so prominent figures representing the first three stages were easy to find. But the fourth stage needed no theorist to drive the movement with ideas; all it needed was people who wouldn't be ashamed to behave in ways that traditional Christianity had always condemned. It was a secularist blow against Christianity, for example, when a young woman openly moved in with her boyfriend. But nobody had to write a book explaining how to do this; all that was needed was a disdain for traditional sexual taboos and a few friends to help with the packing.

Of course there *were* books. There were, for instance, two best-selling books by Dr. Alfred Kinsey (1894-1956) that paved the way for this behavioral secularism: *Sexual Behavior in the Human Male* (1948) and *Sexual Behavior in the Human Female* (1953). Kinsey's books made much sexual conduct that had previously been deemed immoral suddenly seem normal. And in the midst of the sexual revolution there were other best-selling books, rather on the lightweight side: *Sex and the Single Girl* (1962), by Helen Gurley Brown, and *Open Marriage: A New Lifestyle for Couples* (1972), by Nena and George O'Neill. A more heavyweight work was another bestseller, *Human Sexual Response* (1966), by William Masters and Virginia Johnson. But these books — along with scores of others, both fiction and nonfiction, that recommended the delights of sexual freedom — didn't offer theoretical dissuasions from Christianity; what they offered, rather, were incitements to un-Christian behavior.

No doubt such incitements were often effective, but more powerful still were incitements from your peers. If everyone around you was sleeping around, experimenting with new sexual boundaries, why shouldn't you do the same? If many of your married friends were cheating on their spouses, why shouldn't you cheat too? If half the people you knew were leaving their spouses in search of more desirable spouses or lovers, why should you remain in a marriage that was devoid of excitement? If the willful rejection of Christian sexual taboos began with a relatively few pioneers, it soon became a widespread movement that fed upon itself.

To repeat: the cultural/sexual revolution of the 1960s and '70s wasn't a matter of theory, and so I can't offer a theorist as its icon. Further, it was not an *elite* phenomenon, as were the earlier stages of secularism; instead it was a *mass* phenomenon. Eighteenth-century Deism, post–Civil War agnosticism, and John Dewey's aspirations toward benign social engineering all held an appeal for certain kinds of intellectuals, but intellectuals are, almost by definition, never more than a small fraction of a general population. (Even in Athens of the fifth century BC, in Florence of the fifteenth century, or in London of the age of Shakespeare and Francis Bacon and Queen Elizabeth, intellectuals were no more than a small minority.) Thus, Deism, agnosticism, and the ideal of social engineering, although they were meat and potatoes for certain sections of the intellectual elite, were never more than caviar for the general; they never succeeded in winning mass followings. But the behavioral secularism of the fourth and most recent stage was quite a different thing.

After all, you don't have to be an intellectual to get excited by the idea of sexual freedom. *Anybody* can do this, even people without a college degree. The earlier stages were hard slogging for secularists, for they first had to convince people to read (or at least to learn about secondhand) writers such as Voltaire, Kant, Tom Paine, Darwin, Herbert Spencer, Thomas Huxley, the German biblical critics, and John Dewey; and with the exception of Voltaire and Paine, reading these guys is no picnic. But in the fourth stage, the work of the secularist evangelists was far easier. There were no books to read, no exams to take, no subtle concepts to master; all people had to do was liberate themselves from the Puritanical sexual taboos their elders had tried to drill into them since childhood. Secularists from earlier ages had to write big fat books to refute Christianity, but up-to-date modern secularists could accomplish this refutation simply by jumping into bed with a few willing but hitherto illicit partners.

When *Time* magazine makes its annual selection for Person of the Year, occasionally it chooses not an individual or individuals, but an abstract category of person (in 1950, "The American Fighting Man," for example, and in 1975, "American Women"). When I look for a symbol for the fourth stage of secularism — the stage of the sexual revolution and of moral liberalism generally — the best I can do is to point to such an abstract category: the "Baby Boomers." Born in the years following the great hardships of the Depression and World War II, showered by their parents with unconditional affection and an unprecedented abundance of material goods, that pampered and often self-indulgent generation introduced the sexual revolution into American life and, with it, the philosophy of moral liberalism generally.

Appendix III

Liberal Christianity, Fellow-Traveler of Secularism

Although in today's Culture War secularists are the leading enemies of traditional Christianity and the most intense in their anti-Christian values, they're relatively few in number. They wouldn't have much success in furthering their agenda without the help of sympathetic liberal Christians, who, although far less intense in their values, are far more numerous.

The relationship between the two groups is analogous to the relationship that existed more than a half-century ago between the "red" Communist Party of the USA and the "pink" leftists who made up the bulk of the membership and provided the nominal leadership of front groups organized by Communists in the 1930s, '40s, and '50s. Communists provided the ideas and the real leadership, while the fellow-travelers lent support and applause. Practically speaking, in the Culture War, and in the political battles that are byproducts of the Culture War, liberal Christians are the fellow-travelers of the secularists.

Later I'll define *liberal Christianity* by examples and give a brief history of its career in America. Before doing so, however, it might be well if I give an abstract definition of the phenomenon. To do so I'll borrow the words of John Henry Newman in his speech upon receiving the red hat of a cardinal in 1879:

> Liberalism in religion is the doctrine that there is no positive truth in religion, but that one creed is as good as another. . . . It is inconsistent with the recognition of any religion, as *true*. It teaches that all are to be tolerated, for all are matters of opinion. Revealed religion is not a truth, but a sentiment and a taste; not an objective fact, not miraculous; and it is the right of each individual to make it say just what strikes his fancy. . . . Men may go to Protestant churches and to Catholic, may get good from both and belong to neither. They may fraternize together in spiritual thoughts and feelings, without having any view at all of doctrines in common, or seeing the need of them. Since, then, religion is so personal a peculiarity and so private a possession, we must of necessity ignore it in the intercourse of man with man. If a man puts on a new religion every morning, what is that to you?

I'll modify Newman's definition only to say that by *liberalism* in Christianity I mean the strong tendency to arrive at the position outlined above. Someone may be a liberal without totally and expressly abandoning the idea that there's such a thing as religious truth. It's sufficient that he abandon this, that, and the other particular traditional doctrine; soon enough he'll arrive at the view that religious "truth" is of little or no importance. Liberal Christianity is, in essence, the rejection of the dogmatic principle in religion.

Unitarianism: phase one of liberal Protestantism

One of my favorite figures in the history of American religion is William Ellery Channing (1780-1842), the "father of Unitarianism" in America. No doubt one of the reasons I like Channing is that he was a native of my hometown of Newport, where he's still commemorated; but another reason is that he was an admirably good man, on the right side of all the great ethical issues of the day, including slavery, education, temperance, the condition of the working classes, and toleration of Catholic immigrants. Channing's version of Christianity was very "reasonable"; that is, it tossed out many of those elements of Christianity that eighteenth-century rationalism had objected to, most notably the Trinity and the divinity of Christ.

The trouble with Channing's low-dogma religion — apart from the obvious fact that it was a radical departure from historical Christianity — is that it had little or no stability. It wasn't the sort of thing you could very well pass on to your children with doctrine intact; even less could it be expected to reach your grandchildren. Channing and his generation rejected the Trinity but wished to hold on to such beliefs as miracles, a personal God, the uniqueness (although not divinity) of Jesus, and the divine inspiration of the Bible. But for the younger generation, that of Emerson and Theodore Parker, God was no longer personal; Jesus, although a truly great man, was no longer unique; and the Bible, although "inspired," was no more so than the writings of Plato and Shakespeare or the artistic works of Michelangelo. As for miracles — why, everything was a miracle, and therefore nothing was.

When Emerson shocked the older generation of Unitarian divines with his "Divinity School Address" (given in 1838 to the graduating class of his alma mater, the Harvard Divinity School), some of these older Unitarians, although they had been great religious radicals in their own day, tried to check this further advance in radicalism. Harvard professor Andrews Norton (sometimes called "the pope of Unitarianism") wrote a piece called "The

Latest Form of Infidelity" with Emerson and Parker in mind. But it was too late. The younger generation had learned a crucial lesson from the older: reason, not revelation, was the supreme authority; from which it followed that reason (which for Emerson included intuition) was entitled to weigh everything in the balance, including revelation. The only difference between the older and the younger generations was a difference in practice rather than in principle: the latter, not as timid and conservative as the former, applied the purgative power of reason to virtually all Christian dogma.

Eventually, in the twentieth century, Unitarianism would first cease to be a specifically Christian denomination (in its tolerance and open-mindedness, it came to value Buddhism, for example, as equal to Christianity) and later cease to be a theistic religion at all. Unitarianism now had nothing except its name[67] to differentiate it from the Ethical Culture Society. Today it's mainly made up of decent, well-mannered middle- and upper-middle-class people of diverse religious and nonreligious upbringings who rather enjoy going to church on Sunday mornings and who hold no common beliefs — except perhaps that women should have a "right to choose" and gays should be allowed to marry. Two hundred years after Channing and his Boston ministerial colleagues set out to improve Christianity by paring it to its essential content, the denomination they created had so "improved" the old religion as to eliminate its content.

The constant search for religious compromise

My examination of Unitarianism and its history has led me to certain conclusions that I've come to see as applicable to *all* forms

[67] The official name was changed to the Unitarian Universalist Association in 1961 when the Unitarian and Universalist churches merged.

of liberal Protestantism. First, Channing's early Unitarianism was an attempt to find a "middle ground" between traditional Christianity and secularism — in those days, Deism. Unitarians did not, of course, completely embrace the Deists' rationalistic critique of Christianity, but they paid respectful attention to it, lopping off some of the more "irrational" elements of Christianity to make it less vulnerable to the critique. In effect they tried to blend what they saw as the best of Christianity with the best of Deism, thereby producing a hybrid that was supposed to be superior to both its parents. This, I contend, is what liberal Protestantism always does: it attempts to blend Christianity with the form of anti-Christian secularism fashionable at the moment, aiming for a kind of Hegelian synthesis that both preserves and surpasses the earlier thesis and antithesis. In the course of doing this, it drops certain elements — either doctrinal or moral — that traditional Christianity would have considered essential to the religion.

But history teaches that this process of "reforming" Christianity is a slippery slope. Once the principle is established that we're free to reject certain essential elements of classical Christianity, there's no way to limit the operation of this principle. The first generation of Unitarians established the principle by jettisoning the Trinity and the divinity of Christ, and subsequent generations, applying the principle in a more severe way, tossed out nearly everything else. *So it is with all forms of liberal Protestantism*. By reducing, in deference to the critique of Christianity made by the secularism of the day, the dogmatic content of Christianity, it opens the door to further and further reductions of dogmatic content until, given a long enough stretch of time, there will be no dogmatic content left.

There's one other phenomenon that's always connected with the "progress" of liberal Protestantism: the increasing substitution of morality for dogma. On the long road that ends with the end of Christianity, liberal Protestantism more and more comes to see the essence of Christianity to lie in morality.[68] You might have lost all or almost all of your specifically religious beliefs, but if you're still serious about morality, you can say, "Behold, I'm still a Christian." And thus, as religious conviction and intensity decline, moral conviction and intensity tend, at least for a few generations, to increase.

This accounts for the moral earnestness that has always been characteristic of liberal Protestants. Of course, what counts as morality for the liberal might not coincide with what counts as morality for the traditionalist. In Parker's day the traditionalist ranked sobriety, thrift, marital fidelity, and financial honesty at the top of the list of Christian virtues; Parker himself affirmed these virtues and gave special prominence to the fight against slavery. Among latter-day liberal Protestants, moral seriousness might require a commitment to certain causes of social justice, or an earnest concern for public health or the environment; it will also include not merely downplaying but expressly rejecting the traditionalist's concern with abortion and sex.

What this amounts to, for the liberal Protestant, is a Christian moral duty to demolish certain traditional rules of Christian moral duty. From the point of view of classical Christianity, then, liberal Protestantism is a kind of suicide project.

Liberal Protestantism, posing as a "middle way" religion, always has two enemies: secularism on the left and traditional

[68] That great English liberal Protestant, the poet and critic Matthew Arnold, gave classic expression to this attitude when he defined religion as "morality touched with emotion" and God as "the eternal not-ourselves that makes for righteousness."

Protestantism on the right. At some moments it regards secularism as the more serious enemy, but most of the time it views traditional Protestantism as the number-one threat. Furthermore, although liberal Protestantism has always made *some* attempt to persuade secularists to appreciate the merits of Christianity (even if it might happen to be a watered-down version of the religion),[69] mostly its attempts at persuasion have been directed at old-school Protestants and their insufficiently liberal systems of religious belief. As a result, liberal Protestantism is more likely to be found battling its foes on the right than its foes on the left. And in its struggles against religious traditionalism, liberal Protestantism finds it relatively easy to enter into an informal alliance with secularism, for secularism is also engaged in battle against religious traditionalism. Today, as the forces of secularism have become great supporters of the Democratic Party while the forces of traditionalism have become great supporters of the Republican Party, it's easy to see why religious liberals would increasingly lean the Democrats' way.

Modernism: phase two of liberal Protestantism

Unitarianism, as it turned out, never spread much beyond New England, and its Transcendentalist subdivision never got a long way past Concord; but in subtle and gradual ways their influence served to erode the traditional Protestantism of some of America's mainline denominations, especially Congregationalism. The next great leap forward for liberal Protestantism, however, didn't take place until after the Civil War, and the impetus for this came from

[69] See, for instance, the first important work by the greatest of the German liberal theologians, Friedrich Schleiermacher (1768-1834), *On Religion: Speeches to Its Cultured Despisers* (1799).

two intellectual forces across the Atlantic Ocean: from England, the Darwinian theory of evolution; and from Germany, biblical "higher criticism." The same two forces that drove the development of secularist skepticism would open a rift in American Protestantism, setting it upon radically divergent courses.

Darwinism clearly implied that the account of creation given in Genesis was wildly inaccurate and that Protestantism would no longer be able to cling to one of its fundamental beliefs — namely, the inerrancy of the Bible when read literally. German higher criticism, in teaching that many of the traditionally reputed authors (e.g., Moses, David) of the books of the Bible were not in fact the authors, and that much of the content of the Bible was unhistorical and mythical, likewise undermined the belief that the Bible was written under the plenary inspiration of the Holy Spirit.

Some Protestants — the liberals or modernists — embraced higher criticism and Darwinism, and they attempted to reconcile these with their religious beliefs. Following the path cut by Channing, they accomplished this reconciliation not only by discarding those religious beliefs directly contradicted by Darwinian theory and higher criticism, but by adopting a spirit or mentality that was ready to discard still further beliefs, should the results of modern science and scholarship demand it. For these modernists, the dogmatic principle in Christianity was evaporating. No matter how strongly they might be personally attached to the great bulk of traditional Christian beliefs and values, there was, in principle, very little they were unwilling to renounce if modern learning required it. In the century and more that has passed since the beginning of this crisis, later generations of liberals found that they would have to renounce, both in belief and in practice, more and more of the traditional content of Christianity. On the opposite side were the Protestant "fundamentalists," who clung to the old principles of

Protestantism: for example, that the divinely inspired, inerrant Bible is the sole rule of faith, and that salvation comes through faith in Christ alone.[70]

The most dramatic (indeed melodramatic) collision between these two wings of Protestantism took place in Dayton, Tennessee, in the summer of 1925 at the trial of schoolteacher John Scopes: the so-called "Monkey Trial." The actual combatants were the celebrated secularist Clarence Darrow, attorney for the defense, and the great fundamentalist William Jennings Bryan,[71] assisting the prosecution. In this showdown, Protestants of the modernist type were cheering for Darrow the agnostic, not Bryan the Protestant. In other words, they wanted their (traditional) fellow-Christians

[70] The definitive formulation of this point of view is to be found in *The Fundamentals*, a collection (originally published in 1917) of dozens of tracts written and issued in the early years of the twentieth century. A classic account, written from a "fundamentalist" point of view, of the stark contrast between traditional Protestantism and liberal Protestantism is given by J. Gresham Machen in *Christianity and Liberalism* (originally published in 1923; republished by Eerdmans in 1990). Machen argues that liberal Christianity is not a form of Christianity at all; it's a quite different kind of religion that happens to be using an old and very misleading name.

[71] Bryan, in addition to his later fame as a defender of fundamentalism, had been three times the Democratic candidate for president of the United States, losing to McKinley in 1896 (the year young Bryan delivered his famous "Cross of Gold" speech) and 1900 and to Taft in 1908. He later served as Wilson's secretary of state. Poor Bryan! — today he must be spinning in his grave at the secularist takeover of his political party.

defeated, even if such a defeat would, as indeed it did, hand a great victory to secularism.[72] Scopes was convicted and fined for teaching Darwinism in school — a legal victory for the fundamentalists and a legal defeat for the secularists and their modernist allies.[73] But in the far more important court of public opinion, the fundamentalists were trounced. The trial received enormous press coverage, including coverage by that new medium, radio; and to much of the public at large, especially its better-educated sections, the case presented by the fundamentalists seemed nothing other than absurd, a joke. The informal alliance between secularism and Protestantism of the modernist type won a great victory.

At that moment a reasonable person would have predicted the inevitable collapse of fundamentalism. The fundamentalist ship, it seemed, had sprung an irreparable leak, and so it was bound to sink; maybe not overnight, but surely it would sink eventually. Eighty years later, however, it turns out that the reasonable person would have been wrong in his prediction. Protestant fundamentalism has not only survived, but is flourishing. Of course, most of the religious heirs of the earlier fundamentalists no longer call themselves by that name. Many of them call themselves Evangelicals, others Pentecostals, many others simply Christians. But whatever their current labels, they make up the anti-liberal or anti-modernist wing of American Protestantism. And their pews

[72] For an account of the Scopes trial, see the book that won the Pulitzer Prize for history in 1998, Edward J. Larson's *Summer for the Gods* (Basic Books, 1997). Also worth seeing is the old movie *Inherit the Wind* (1960), a fictionalized version of the trial, with Spencer Tracy playing the Darrow-based character and Frederick March the Bryan-based character.

[73] Later the conviction was reversed by the Tennessee Supreme Court.

are packed with eager believers (as are those of certain other anti-modernist Christian churches that are perhaps not entitled, strictly speaking, to be called Protestant — notably, Mormonism and the Jehovah's Witnesses) while the modernist or "mainline" liberal Protestant churches (for example, Episcopal, Presbyterian, Methodist) are in steep numerical decline.[74]

The Social Gospel: phase three of liberal Protestantism

I've argued that liberal Protestantism always tries to occupy a middle ground between traditional Protestantism and the secularism of the day, whatever that happens to be. In this way Unitarianism was a response to Deism, and Protestant modernism a response to late-nineteenth-century agnosticism. And in response to Dewey-ism or Progressive secularism, that is, to the social-reconstruction kind of secularism that flourished in the Progressive and New Deal eras, we find the "Social Gospel" movement — as typified above all in the career and writings of the Baptist pastor Walter Rauschenbusch (1861-1918), born just three years after Dewey.[75] Moved by his experiences in ministering to the

[74] The classic work on the decline of the mainline churches and the growth of the conservative churches was written more than thirty years ago by Dean M. Kelley, *Why Conservative Churches Are Growing* (Harper and Row, 1972). A later and very worthwhile book that insightfully discusses the same theme is Roger Finke and Rodney Stark's *The Churching of America, 1776-1990: Winners and Losers in Our Religious Economy* (Rutgers University Press, 1992).

[75] Rauschenbusch's best-known book is *Christianity and the Social Crisis* (1908), but he wrote a number of other books in the Social Gospel genre, among them *Christianizing the Social Order* (1912), *The Social Principles of Jesus* (1916), and *A Theology for the Social Gospel* (1917).

poor, and influenced theologically by higher criticism, Rauschenbusch devised a Christian social ethic that aimed at instituting on earth the heavenly kingdom of God.

By the beginning of the twentieth century, it was clear that American society had entered a period of great social crisis. In the half-century between the Civil War and the First World War, the United States had been rapidly transformed from a predominantly rural-agricultural nation into a predominantly urban-industrial nation. Immensely wealthy and powerful capitalists (the so-called "robber barons") had emerged; a great population shift from country to city had taken place; many millions of southern- and eastern-European immigrants had arrived, settling mostly in those big cities. Black Americans, ex-slaves and the children of ex-slaves, were struggling to create a post-emancipation life for themselves in a South that was racially segregated both by custom and by law. And politics at all levels — local, state, and national — had become corrupt on a large scale.

Where Dewey and other nonreligious thinkers (many of them sociologists and economists) responded by offering secularist-utopian solutions to the social crisis, Rauschenbusch and others in his movement offered Christian solutions. As they saw things, American Protestantism had concentrated too exclusively on the salvation of the individual soul — which was an important thing, to be sure, but not the *only* important thing, for society too had to be "saved." To save society, Christianity had to modify its theretofore individualistic, otherworldly focus and give true social application to the love-thy-neighbor ethic taught by Jesus, using its energies and resources to combat social ills such as poverty, violence, prejudice, labor injustice, and drunkenness.

The Social Gospel movement illustrates the liberal Protestantism rule that I've already spoken of — namely, that as doctrinal content declines, moral intensity increases. Modernism, the second phase of American liberal Protestantism, had reduced the doctrinal content of Christianity; no sooner was this done than the Social Gospel movement arrived, full of moral earnestness. The movement followed the lead of its forbears in further reducing Christianity's dogmatic content, for in exalting the significance of social betterment, many of its followers depreciated the traditional importance of individual salvation.[76]

I've said a number of times that the perennial modus operandi of liberal Christianity in America (and not just in America) has been to find a middle ground between traditional Christianity and secularism. And since secularism tends to move ever further from the traditional Christian worldview, while traditional Christianity moves hardly at all, in order to maintain that desired middle ground, liberal Christianity must also move ever further away from traditional Christianity. Thus, over time, it tends to retain less and less of its former moral and dogmatic content.

Of course, liberal Christians don't like the suggestion that they're departing from true Christianity, and they usually defend themselves by making a distinction between the "essential" content of Christianity and its "incidental," or nonessential, content.

[76] This cannot, however, be said of Rauschenbusch himself, who held that a Christian concern with social reform did not in any degree release us from a concern with individual salvation; rather a concern for our soul and a concern for our society perfectly complement one another. A book that nicely shows both sides of Rauschenbusch's concerns is *Walter Rauschenbusch: Selected Writings*, edited by Winthrop S. Hudson (Paulist Press, 1984).

In the manner of the early Protestant Reformers (Luther, Calvin, et al.), but going far beyond them, liberal Christians say that, by discarding inessential doctrines and rules, they're not moving farther from true Christianity but in fact closer to it; by removing the tarnish of unnecessary dogma, they're allowing the true essence of Christianity to shine through more brilliantly than ever.

Get rid of the Trinity, and you allow the truth of monotheism to shine through. Redefine unto oblivion the divinity of Christ, and you allow the greatness of the man Jesus to shine through. De-emphasize individual salvation in the afterlife, and you allow the glory of God's kingdom in this life to shine through. Soften the taboos on contraception and abortion, and you allow the dignity of the female half of the human race to shine through. Overturn the biblical injunction against homosexuality, and you allow the rainbow-like diversity of God's creation to shine through.

Since my aim here is to describe liberal Christianity, not to evaluate it, I won't judge whether there's merit in the liberal distinction between Christianity's essential and nonessential content. I will say only this: that Christianity has been in the world a long time, nearly two thousand years; that during almost all this time, almost all Christians subscribed to a belief system that included all the teachings of the Nicene and Chalcedonian creeds and to a system of morality that prohibited non-marital sex, abortion, homosexuality, and suicide; and that orthodox Catholics and traditional Protestants, whatever their many disagreements on other points, have always been in agreement on these doctrinal and moral beliefs. Somebody might argue that liberal Christianity is a *better* religion than orthodox Christianity, but nobody can deny that liberal Christianity is *different* from the Christianity that has existed through most of twenty centuries.

Liberal Protestantism today: phase four

The most recent leftward lurch of American liberal Protestantism began during — and as a result of — the great American cultural revolution of the 1960s and '70s. As we've seen, this revolution was inspired by the Personal Liberty Principle (PLP) and the Tolerance Principle (TP), and it was especially characterized by a great amount of sexual permissiveness, the so-called sexual revolution. This cultural revolution represented a new stage for secularism, differing from the earlier stages in two respects: its attack on Christianity wasn't confined to intellectuals, but was a mass movement; and it wasn't merely an attack on the doctrinal beliefs of Christianity, but on Christian *morality*, especially its sexual morality. As we saw in the previous chapter, this kind of secularism continues to the present, and has become firmly allied with the Democratic Party.

Now, we'd expect that liberal Protestantism — that middle-way religion — would, with some moderation, mimic this "fourth stage" secularism. More specifically, we'd expect that up-to-date liberal Protestantism would make a significant retreat from the traditional principles of Christian sexual morality. And sure enough, this is exactly what happened. Liberal Protestants accepted, or at least half-accepted, the sexual revolution, and today they condone or tolerate fornication, unmarried cohabitation, homosexual conduct, and abortion — although they do so, as befits their attempt to stake out a middle path, in a less overt and enthusiastic way than do typical secularists. They say, for example, that cohabitation and homosexual relationships, to merit Christian approbation, should involve some significant degree of "commitment." They say that women should have abortions for good reasons only, and only after they've devoted serious thought and prayer to the subject. For all intents and purposes, today's liberal Protestantism embraces the general principles of secularist moral liberalism, only slightly softened in practice and sprinkled with Christian poetry and music.

The landmark book that marked the beginning of this latest stage of liberal Protestantism was *Situation Ethics: The New Morality*, published in 1966 by an Episcopal priest named Joseph Fletcher. Compared with the conduct liberal Protestantism is willing to endorse today, forty years later, Fletcher's ideas were tame. Although he allowed for the moral permissibility in some cases of fornication, abortion, homosexuality, and even adultery, he did so only in very extreme situations. His most important contribution to the rise of the latest form of liberal Christianity wasn't his rejection of the sinfulness of certain acts, but rather his dismissal of the traditional Christian idea of absolute moral rules — of exceptionless moral norms. In classical Christianity there are numerous absolutes — never commit murder, never commit abortion, never commit suicide, never commit fornication, never commit adultery, never commit homosexual acts — but for Fletcher there was only one absolute: "Love your neighbor." This absolute, he said, trumps all other rules of morality. Provided your conduct is an act of genuine love, you're free in theory to commit fornication, abortion, adultery — and presumably, even murder, not to mention lying, cheating, and stealing — with a clean conscience.

At the moment, the contest between liberal and classical Protestantism is seriously dividing a number of major Protestant denominations, including Presbyterians, Methodists, and Episcopalians. The 2004 ordination of Gene Robinson, an openly homosexual man, as bishop of New Hampshire has brought the Episcopal Church in the United States to the point of virtual schism.

Probably the best-known icon of liberal Protestantism in recent times has been the retired Episcopal Bishop of Newark, New Jersey, John Shelby Spong, who has taken religious liberalism just about as far as it can be taken — to a conclusion that is simultaneously logical and absurd. Spong's many writings occupy prime space on the religion shelves of bookstores. His appeal is to persons who want to be Christians and non-Christians at the same time, for he rejects every article of the Nicene Creed. In fact, he has taken the trouble to write books devoted to the rejection of this or that article of the Creed: the Virgin Birth *(Born of a Woman)* and the Resurrection *(Resurrection: Myth or Reality?)*, to name two. He even goes so far as to reject the Creed's first and most basic article: belief in God. (At all events, he says he believes in a "non-theistic" God, which is rather like believing in a non-circular circle.) Needless to say, he's also very *au courant* in matters of sexuality.

Nothing distinguishes Spong from the outright secularist other than the bishop's rather odd notion that he believes in God and is a Christian. All liberal Christians are similarly engaged in some degree of self-deception, working at destroying Christianity while convincing themselves that they're faithful Christians, but in this game Spong wins the blue ribbon. It might be objected, therefore, that I've been guilty of taking a cheap shot at religious liberalism by offering Spong as an example, his case being so extreme. To this charge I plead guilty, as far as it goes. But I do believe that Spong, ridiculous as he is, has simply arrived more quickly than most at the terminus toward which all Christian liberalism tends.

Liberal Catholicism

Until the 1960s, liberal Christianity was virtually non-existent in the Catholic Church in America. It might have been present among many American Catholics as a *feeling* or *attitude*, and there might have been back-room arguments presented in its defense, but almost nobody was advocating its principles in public lectures or in print. Prior to the 1960s, the people called "liberal Catholics" weren't theologically liberal or anti-dogmatic; hence, they weren't liberal Christians according to the definition I've been using in this book. Rather, these people were liberal in the sense that they disagreed with the autocratic style typical of many persons who occupied positions of authority in the Church, from the pope and bishops down to local mothers superior; and also in the sense that they disagreed with the rightist political views of many in the Church hierarchy — for example, the widespread clerical applause given to General Franco in Spain despite Franco's commission of mass murder during the Spanish Civil War and the strongly authoritarian dictatorship he established in Spain afterward.

To be a "liberal" Catholic before the 1960s meant little more than this: that you were a great fan of Franklin Roosevelt and the AFL and CIO, that you were strongly opposed to anti-Semitism and racism, that you believed Franco to be a scoundrel, that you made fun of bishops who adopted a pompous episcopal style, and that you had disdain for the small-mindedness and narrow-mindedness that commonly characterized Catholic college education. Your liberalism had nothing to do with questioning the Incarnation or the Virgin Birth or the Real Presence in the Eucharist; and it certainly had nothing to do with challenging the ancient Christian taboos on fornication, homosexual conduct, and abortion; it didn't even have to do with agitating for married or women priests.

In the wake of Vatican II, the situation changed suddenly and thoroughly — and not simply because of the council.[77] Overnight,

[77] For an account of the reasons for this change, see part 1 of *The Decline and Fall of the Catholic Church in America.*

as it were, large sections of American Catholicism moved into the theretofore all-Protestant ranks of liberal Christianity. This was part of a liberal religion movement sweeping over the Catholic world in Europe and Latin America as well as in the United States and Canada.

An indication of the American Catholic turn toward religious liberalism came on July 25, 1968, when Pope Paul VI promulgated his profoundly controversial encyclical, *Humanae Vitae*, which reiterated, reinforced, and elaborated on the traditional Catholic condemnation of artificial contraception. Prior to the appearance of the encyclical there had been a widespread expectation among liberal Catholics that the Vatican was about to relax the Church's traditional ban on contraception; indeed, a papal commission two years before had recommended just such a relaxation. An explosion of rejection followed the promulgation of the encyclical. The most conspicuous incident of that explosion came within just a few days, when more than two hundred Catholic theologians took out a full-page ad in the *New York Times* expressing their dissent from the papal teaching. An even bigger explosion took place underground, as it were, as millions of Catholic contraception-practicing married couples decided that the pope, and by extension, the Church, was plainly wrong on birth control and out of touch with the realities of modern married life. Many parish priests did little to discourage this attitude, and some even privately condoned their actions by assuring them that their "voice of conscience" was more authoritative than the voice of the Vatican. Many others simply stayed silent, in effect tacitly condoning the practice of contraception by not objecting to it. Few came to the aid of the pope.

What was being rejected here, of course, wasn't just the ancient birth-control taboo but papal authority itself; in fact, the very teaching authority of the Church. If one authoritative teaching could be ignored in good conscience, others could be ignored too. Soon it became clear that many, perhaps even most, of the members of the Catholic Church in the United States were what came to be called "cafeteria Catholics" or "à la carte Catholics" — picking and choosing which teachings of the Church to accept.

Except in name, "cafeteria Catholicism" is barely distinguishable in principle from liberal Protestantism. But in practice there remains one significant difference: despite the infiltration of liberal Christianity into the Church, American liberal Catholicism has never been quite as liberal as American liberal Protestantism. This isn't surprising, since Catholics got into the game later and haven't yet had time to travel so far.

More important, at the summit of the strongly hierarchical Catholic Church — at the level of the pope and his thousands of bishops, including many hundreds in the United States — it's very difficult for doctrinal liberalism to make a breakthrough. Bishops, as everyone knows, can easily be incompetent or irresponsible, but it's less easy for them to be doctrinally liberal. For the pope is still Catholic, and if priests exhibit clear tendencies in the direction of religious liberalism, they're unlikely to be promoted by Rome to bishop in the first place; and if these tendencies manifest themselves only after they become bishops, they probably won't advance further in the hierarchy. These orthodox bishops, in turn, have great authority over the diocesan priests who serve under them.

For all that, it remains true that liberal Christianity has made considerable progress among American Catholics in the last four decades. This can be seen to varying degrees among the clergy and in religious orders, but most of all among the laity. Who will deny that the great majority of American lay Catholics have accepted the traditional Protestant principle of *private judgment* — or more exactly, that they've accepted a latter-day and secularized version of this principle? Originally the principle meant that, the Bible being the sole rule of faith, the individual Christian has the right to arrive at his own interpretation of the Bible and its parts; he isn't obliged to accept interpretations delivered to him by popes, bishops, or even his local priest or minister. But according to the original principle — and this is still observed by classical Protestants today — private judgment is rightly exercised only in a way that isn't arbitrary or capricious; in other words, the Christian should read the Bible with great care, with earnest prayer, and with at least respectful attention to the interpretations that have been given to it by Christians who are more expert than himself (his local pastor, for example). The idea is that the Holy Spirit, who inspired the writers of Scripture, will also guide the reader who is rightly disposed.

In contrast, what I called the "latter-day and secularized version of this principle" says that the individual has a perfect right, and perhaps even an obligation, to "think for himself" on just about all topics — not only when it comes to the Bible, but on nearly every question of religion, morality, politics, dress, manners, fine and popular arts, sports, food, drink, and so on. In most matters it isn't the verdict of authorities or the weight of tradition that is to be given the highest regard; rather it is one's personal opinion.

But in Catholicism there's little room for "private judgment" regarding the Bible or Christian doctrine generally. The Church's official teachers and authorities on doctrine and the Bible are the bishops, above all the Bishop of Rome; and not just the bishops and pope who happen to be alive and in office today, but the long succession of bishops and popes (as well as the theologians whose work they sanctioned) going back to the Apostles. The Catholic theory is that the good Catholics, when it comes to doctrine and the Bible, will assent to the official verdicts and formulations of the Church, not pick and choose among them according to their private judgments. Quite obviously there's a strong incompatibility between this traditional Catholic idea and the American idea that every person should think for himself. But most American Catholics today are more American than they are Catholic, and when these two parts of their identity clash with one another, as they do on this matter of private judgment, it isn't surprising that the American part usually wins out.

The most conspicuous example of this is, of course, the widespread dismissal of Catholic teaching on contraception. But there have been other examples of widespread rejection in recent decades: rejection of the rule against premarital sex, of the teaching on homosexuality, of the rule banning female priests, and of the rule against abortion. How widespread is the rejection of traditional doctrines having to do with topics other than morality — the Trinity, the divinity of Christ, the Virgin Birth, the Resurrection, the Real Presence in the Eucharist? This isn't clear, but I suspect that rejections of this kind are also fairly widespread. Anecdotal evidence suggests as much.

By embracing a liberal or non-orthodox version of their religion, liberal Catholics, like their liberal Protestant brothers and sisters, have in effect made themselves available as allies and fellow travelers of anti-Christian secularism. Usually without realizing what they're doing, liberal Catholics, like liberal Protestants, have been enlisted to give aid and comfort to secularism in its great anti-Christianity crusade. On matters political and cultural, liberal Catholics, like liberal Protestants, tend to find themselves more in sympathy with secularists on their left than with their traditional co-religionists on the right. And since secularism now plays a dominant role in the national Democratic Party, it follows that liberal Catholics would provide — and in fact are currently providing — a significant share of money, work, and votes for the national Democratic Party. Liberal Catholics too are unwittingly aiding the very forces that seek their Church's destruction.

Appendix IV

The Father of Catholic Excuses: Mario Cuomo at Notre Dame

The excuses and justifications for supporting abortion given by garden-variety Catholic Democratic politicians (many of them discussed in chapter 5) weren't good enough for Mario Cuomo, former Governor of New York,[78] who's not only more intellectual than virtually all his co-religionist fellow politicians but also the owner of an intellect formed on Catholic principles. So when Cuomo set out to defend the right of a Catholic politician to be pro-choice, in a September 13, 1984, speech at the University of Notre Dame, he offered an argument that was more polished and sophisticated than any heard before. His abortion-and-politics speech immediately became a classic, a touchstone for all pro-choice Catholic public figures.

The speech was especially timely because another Catholic politician from New York was on the ballot that fall as Democratic presidential candidate Walter Mondale's running-mate:

[78] Cuomo was elected governor in 1982 and served until defeated by George Pataki in 1994.

Rep. Geraldine Ferraro from Queens. Although she said she was "personally opposed" to abortion, Ferraro had a pro-choice voting record in Congress (otherwise, of course, she couldn't have been on the ticket, since by 1984 the abortion folks already had a sufficient grip on the Democratic Party to be able to veto any presidential or vice-presidential candidate who wasn't "safe" on their issue). During the campaign Ferraro attracted a lot of flak because of her apparently inconsistent — and obviously un-Catholic — abortion position, most notably from the newly appointed archbishop of New York, John Cardinal O'Connor. She had contended that there was more than one legitimate Catholic position on abortion, but O'Connor contradicted her very publicly.

In his speech at Notre Dame, Cuomo was in effect coming to Ferraro's defense, even though he didn't mention her name. He didn't need to; everybody in the audience understood the subtext. But he was doing much more than that: he was laying down a general rule for Catholic politicians in the United States, a rule that said that Catholic elected officials mustn't allow their bishops, or even the pope, to determine their political stance on abortion. Cuomo's speech made perfect sense to moral liberals. It made perfect sense to them that Catholics should disregard their Church's teaching that abortion is a grave injustice and should instead adopt one of the key beliefs of moral liberalism. In other words, despite its Catholic setting and its Catholic ornamentation, Governor Cuomo's speech was in its essence a moral liberal's manifesto.

In the course of his eloquent speech, Cuomo made it clear that he's a believing Catholic — not a dissenter from orthodoxy on the question of abortion or any other life question:

> As a Catholic I respect the teaching authority of the bishops. . . . I accept the church's teaching on abortion. . . . As

> a Catholic, I have accepted certain answers as the right ones for myself and my family, and because I have, they have influenced me in special ways, as Matilda's husband, as a father of five children, as a son who stood next to his own father's deathbed trying to decide if the tubes and needles no longer served a purpose.

Cuomo proceeds to offer a fourfold defense of the right of a Catholic politician to support pro-choice public policies despite his pro-life religious convictions.

• *The pluralism defense*. "I protect my right to be a Catholic," he says, "by preserving your right to believe as a Jew, a Protestant, or nonbeliever, or as anything else you choose. We know that the price of seeking to force our belief on others is that they might someday force theirs on us."

As an American, I'm free, Cuomo grants, to press for a law banning abortion. "But should I? Is it helpful? Is it essential to human dignity? Does it promote harmony and understanding? Or does it divide us so fundamentally that it threatens our ability to function as a pluralistic society?" He answers these questions by saying, "Our public morality . . . depends on a consensus view of right and wrong. The values derived from religious belief will not — and should not — be accepted as part of the public morality unless they are shared by the pluralistic community at large, by consensus."

This answer has a number of defects. First, although he doesn't precisely (or even approximately) define how broad a "consensus" has to be to qualify as a consensus, Cuomo seems to have something like this in mind: that any group constituting a good-size or important minority in society has in effect the right to exercise a veto. Hence, the presence of secularists, almost all of whom support a legal right to abortion, and liberal Christians, most of whom support such a right, would be enough to establish that there's no "consensus" in the United States in favor of abortion-restriction legislation.

But by this standard, Cuomo would have to say that the Civil Rights Act of 1964 was illegitimate since it wasn't based on a "consensus" — being strongly opposed by white racists, who certainly at the time constituted a good-size and important minority in American society. And for the same reason, the Supreme Court's *Brown v. Board of Education* ruling of 1954 would have to be judged illegitimate. And so would the Court's 1973 *Roe v. Wade* decision, since at the time the decision was handed down, almost all religious conservatives — Catholics, Protestants, Mormons, Orthodox Jews, and others — disapproved of the ruling. Ironically, using his "there must be a consensus" standard, Cuomo should have denounced as illegitimate the Court decision that created the legal right to abortion that he was now defending as public policy.

Second, while Cuomo insists that Catholics have no right to create a "public morality" that includes values not accepted on a consensus basis, he doesn't apply this rule the other way around: he doesn't equally insist that *secularists* have no right to create a public morality that includes values not accepted on a consensus basis. Secularists don't accept anti-abortion values; hence, says Cuomo, Catholics mustn't make anti-abortion values part of our public morality. But he has no objection when secularists (with the very generous help of the U.S. Supreme Court) make pro-abortion values part of our public morality. The fact is, public morality can't possibly be neutral on the matter of abortion: it will, to some degree or other, be either pro-abortion or anti-abortion. Cuomo, no matter how sincerely anti-abortion he might be in his private religious convictions, favors a pro-abortion public morality.

Besides, Cuomo's argument takes for granted that American pluralism is of what may be called the *absolute* kind, whereas in fact it's only *relative*. Pro-pluralism Americans aren't prepared to tolerate *all* forms of cultural diversity. Would our cultural pluralists be willing to tolerate, for instance, the grisly practice of female genital mutilation, which in certain parts of Africa is culturally mandated? After all, in recent decades, migration to the United States from Africa has notably increased, so it's increasingly likely that there will be African immigrants living in America who approve of this practice. Or are American pluralists ready to tolerate another idea held by many recent immigrants — that men are entitled by nature to outrank women in society and the family and are entitled, if need be, to enforce that social superiority with force?

Of course not. Except for a small number of exceptions among the multiculturalist lunatic fringe, it's clear that the champions of pluralism don't favor absolute pluralism; they won't, in the name of pluralism, allow those who favor genital mutilation or male supremacy to veto American cultural rules banning such things.

But if poor and relatively uneducated immigrant groups aren't entitled to veto certain values that the majority of Americans prefer, why should a pro-choice minority have a greater entitlement? Why should they be entitled to veto the anti-abortion will of the majority in, say, South Dakota? If the people of South Dakota, acting through their elected officials, wished to ban abortion, why shouldn't they be free to do so, just as they're free to ban female genital mutilation and male supremacy?

Cuomo's "pluralism" argument hinges on the principle of absolute pluralism — a principle that virtually nobody believes in, including Mario Cuomo.

• *The practicality-and-prudence defense*. Cuomo has no doubt that abortion is contrary to the moral law. Neither does he have any doubt that Catholics ought to try to reduce the number of abortions in the United States. But how best to do this — according to Cuomo, that's the important question. When bishops teach Catholics that abortion is wrong, they speak with legitimate authority. However, he said, recommending political strategies based on that teaching is something else. When it came to battling moral evils, American bishops have traditionally been pragmatic and prudential. Cuomo notes how in the pre–Civil War period, for example, they didn't denounce slavery. This wasn't because they held slavery to be morally permissible; rather, it was because they made a prudential judgment that denouncing it would serve no useful purpose — indeed, it might even cause harm. Cuomo says he'd like to see the bishops observe a similar reticence when it comes to abortion, for legal bans on abortion are not practical and therefore are imprudent.

> I believe [he says] that legal interdicting of all abortions by either the federal government or the individual states is not a plausible possibility and, even if it could be obtained, it wouldn't work. Given present attitudes, it would be Prohibition revisited, legislating what couldn't be enforced and in the process creating a disrespect for law in general.

Cuomo is quite obviously correct that it would be impossible in practice to pass an amendment to the United States Constitution banning abortion. It was a political impossibility at the time he made his Notre Dame speech, and it remains so today. But is it impossible to ban abortion in individual states? It might have been, and might still be today, impossible in his own state of New York, and in other states in the Northeast and on the West Coast. But even in these "impossible" states, a strong case can be made for *attempting* to enact anti-abortion laws. The proposed legislation might not pass, at least not for many years, but the legislative and public debates surrounding such proposals could well serve a useful educational purpose. Such would not be the first time that unsuccessful legislative attempts gradually enlightened the public.

What about the "red" states? Even in 1984, many of those states would have been able to enact strong anti-abortion laws if the Court's *Roe* decision had not stood in their way. And certainly they would be able to do so today, especially when the Republican Party, an anti-abortion party, is far more powerful in the South than it was in 1984. Should *Roe* be overturned in the near future, there can be little doubt that many states — and not just in the South[79] — would rush to enact abortion-restriction legislation.

And what about Cuomo's contention that laws banning abortion couldn't be enforced? He makes this assertion without defending it — other than to suggest comparisons with Prohibition-era speakeasies and bootleggers. I'll discuss the practicality of enforcement later, but for now let me just say this: in the 1920s, it was far easier to sneak an illegal drink during Prohibition than it would be to sneak an illegal abortion in twenty-first-century Alabama. It's true enough that a haphazardly enforced law against abortion in the state of New York might create "disrespect for law in general," but would a reasonably well-enforced law in Alabama have the same effect? More important, if he's concerned about how bad law can create disrespect for law in general, why does Cuomo not mention the disrespect generated by the *Roe v. Wade* decision? Hasn't

[79] In February of 2006, South Dakota passed a very strict anti-abortion law (permitting abortion only to save the life of the mother) in hopes that this law would lead to a Supreme Court reconsideration of *Roe*.

the cultural divide over that decision served to undermine respect for the Supreme Court and for courts in general — and worse still, for the Constitution?

• *Catholic shortcomings/hypocrisy*. It ill befits Catholics, says Cuomo, to demand anti-abortion laws when they themselves are so "soft" on abortion:

> Catholics, the statistics show, support the right to abortion in equal proportion to the rest of the population. Despite the teaching in our homes and schools and pulpits, despite the sermons and pleadings of parents and priests and prelates, despite all the effort at defining our opposition to the sin of abortion, collectively we Catholics apparently believe — and perhaps act — little differently from those who don't share our commitment.
>
> Are we asking government to make criminal what we believe to be sinful because we ourselves can't stop committing the sin? The failure here is not Caesar's. This failure is our failure, the failure of the entire people of God.
>
> Nobody has expressed this better than a bishop in my own state, Joseph Sullivan. . . . "The major problem the church has is internal," the bishop said last month in reference to abortion. "How do we teach? As much as I think we're responsible for advocating public policy issues, our primary responsibility is to teach our own people. We haven't done that. We're asking politicians to do what we haven't done effectively ourselves."
>
> I agree with the bishop. . . . Unless we Catholics . . . set an example that is clear and compelling, then we will never convince this society to change the civil laws to protect what we preach is precious human life.

For the most part, any Catholic can say, "Amen!" to this. Yet Cuomo (committing what logic textbooks call "the fallacy of division") speaks as though *all* Catholics exhibit the softness on abortion that's exhibited by the "average" Catholic. He fails to note that when it comes to abortion there is found among American Catholics something that statisticians call a bimodal distribution. Some (let's call them "orthodox Catholics") strongly adhere to traditional Church teaching; they regard abortion as unwarranted homicide and judge America's abortion regime to be a system of mass killing of innocents. Others (let's call them "cafeteria Catholics") have "conformed themselves to the world." They find abortion to be a tolerable practice, often indulging in it themselves. Throw the two kinds of Catholics together and average their scores, and it turns out that the average Catholic is just about as tolerant of abortion as the average American. But does this mean that orthodox Catholics must strictly abstain from seeking anti-abortion legislation because their "cafeteria" co-religionists condone abortion? This hardly seems reasonable or fair — yet this is what Cuomo is arguing.

• *The decency of pro-choicers*. Not everyone, Cuomo points out, agrees with the Catholic view of abortion:

> And those who don't — those who endorse legalized abortions — aren't a ruthless, callous alliance of anti-Christians determined to overthrow our moral standards. In many cases, the proponents of legal abortion are the very people who have worked with Catholics to realize the goals of social justice set out in papal encyclicals: the American Lutheran Church, the Central Conference of American Rabbis, the Presbyterian Church in the United States, B'nai B'rith Women, the Women of the Episcopal Church.

> These are just a few of the religious organizations that don't share the church's position on abortion.

Only two brief comments are necessary here. One is that the religious organizations listed here are all "liberal": some liberal Christian, others liberal Jewish. And liberal religion, if the argument I made earlier in the book is sound, is an ally of secularism, a fellow-traveler assisting secularism in its opposition to all forms of traditional Christianity, including Catholicism.

The other comment is this: I grant that those who endorse legalized abortion are not "ruthless" and "callous." For the most part, they're well-educated, well-mannered, upper-middle-class people who make for pleasant company if you happen to find yourself in their midst. But as I've argued throughout this book, and contrary to what Mario Cuomo told his audience at Notre Dame, they *do* constitute an "alliance of anti-Christians determined to overthrow our [Catholic] moral standards." This wasn't as clear in 1984 as it is today, but it's surprising that a shrewd observer like Mario Cuomo wouldn't have seen this even that early in the day.

Traditional Catholic reasons for tolerating moral evils

So much for the points made in Cuomo's famous speech. But the speech was important not so much for its actual arguments as for evoking a couple of themes that have a larger significance. One of these is the great American ideal of separation of church and state; the other is the traditional Catholic idea that there are some moral evils that society should tolerate. The first of these themes I treated in the "separation of church and state" excuse. The second theme I'll discuss here.

What does Catholic thought say about the legitimacy and propriety of Catholics "imposing" their rules of morality on the non-Catholic section of society? Well, it all depends: it depends upon the rules in question and upon the situation. In examining this question, let's first make a distinction between two categories of rules: Church-made law and Natural Law.

There are some rules of conduct that are made by Church authorities and capable of being repealed by the same authorities; for example, the rule that was in place until the 1960s, "Don't eat meat on Fridays," or the current rule, "Don't eat meat on Fridays in Lent." Such rules apply only to Catholics, not to non-Catholics. To violate a rule of this kind is to perform an act that is *malum prohibitum* — an act that isn't wrong in itself *(malum in se)* but wrong purely and simply because it's forbidden by a competent authority.

There's another kind of rule — the kind stemming from Natural Law — the violation of which would constitute a *malum in se*. Some examples of this kind of rule would be "Do not commit murder," "Do not commit adultery," and "Do not steal." These are not, according to the Catholic view of things, man-made or Church-made mores. And since they're not *made* by the Church, they can't be *repealed* by the Church. Rules of conduct of this kind don't have to be called "Natural Law," but that's the customary name for them in the Catholic theological and philosophical tradition. The idea here is that there's an unwritten and not-man-made moral law binding not just on Catholics but on all human beings regardless of race, religion, sex, country, or century.[80]

[80] See Cicero's classic description of this law in his *Republic*: "There is in fact a true law — namely, right reason — which is in accordance with nature, applies to all men, and is unchangeable and eternal. By its commands this

No Catholic, not even the pope (or perhaps I should say, especially not the pope), thinks it would be right for Catholics to impose the former of these two kinds of rules, the Church-made kind, on non-Catholics. The most devout and doctrinaire Catholic in the United States Senate would never think to propose a bill banning the consumption of meat on Fridays in Lent. But rules against abortion (for example) are *not* of this nature. According to the Catholic view, abortion is a violation of Natural Law, hence wrong for everyone, not just Catholics.

It doesn't necessarily follow from this, however, that abortion should be made illegal; according to the Catholic view, not *all* violations of Natural Law should be prohibited by law. Thomas Aquinas, a good Catholic authority on the relationship between morality and legislation if ever there was one, once asked the question: "Whether it belongs to human law [i.e., manmade law] to repress all vices" — to which he gave a negative answer. "Human law," he said, "does not prohibit all vices from which the virtuous

> law summons men to the performance of their duties; by its prohibitions it restrains them from doing wrong. Its commands and prohibitions always influence good men, but are without effect upon the bad. To invalidate this law by human legislation is never morally right, nor is it permissible ever to restrict its operation, and to annul it wholly is impossible. . . . It will not lay down one rule at Rome and another at Athens, nor will it be one rule today and another tomorrow. But there will be one law, eternal and unchangeable, binding at all times upon all peoples; and there will be, as it were, one common master and ruler of men, namely, God, who is the author of this law, its interpreter, and its sponsor. . . . Out of all the material of the philosophers' discussions, surely there comes nothing more valuable than the full realization that we are born for Justice, and that right is based, not upon man's opinions, but upon Nature."

abstain but only the more serious ones, from which it is possible for the majority to abstain, and especially those which are harmful to others and which, if not prohibited, would make the preservation of human society impossible. Thus human law prohibits murders, thefts, and the like."[81] Catholic teaching, for instance, considers masturbation to be contrary to Natural Law, but since it isn't "harmful to others" in any socially significant way, no Catholic legislator should consider it his duty to enact anti-masturbation statutes. But since abortion clearly harms another, directly and gravely, this exception doesn't apply.

So far, then, we've seen that the rule against abortion isn't merely a Church-made rule; nor can we say that abortion, although forbidden by Natural Law, isn't harmful to others. But still it doesn't necessarily follow that abortion should be prohibited by legislation, for Catholicism has yet another category of *malum in se* that shouldn't be legislated against. Perhaps abortion will fall under this exception. Let's take a look at it.

Some conceivable laws, although they would ban something that's prohibited by Natural Law and harmful to others, shouldn't be enacted because they'd be either ineffective or counterproductive. For example: adultery is a violation of Natural Law and significantly harmful to others (certainly the spouse of the adulterer, probably his children, and likely society at large). But laws against adultery would be largely unenforceable. They might have been enforceable in a society made up mainly of small villages in which everybody knows everybody else's business (early Massachusetts, for example, the setting of Hawthorne's *The Scarlet Letter*); but they wouldn't be enforceable in twenty-first-century America. Worse, they might invite abuses: blackmail, invasions of privacy,

[81] *Summa Theologica*, I-II, Q. 96, art. 2.

and so forth. Another example: many Catholic societies have historically tolerated prostitution — and this without objection from Church authorities — on the grounds that this is a vice which, given the customs (or culture) of the societies concerned, was practically impossible to eradicate. In such societies, laws against prostitution would be ineffective, hence not worth enacting.

Does this exception apply to abortion in the United States? Would laws prohibiting abortion be ineffective or counterproductive? Very probably not. Such laws would almost certainly be targeted, not at the women undergoing abortion, but at those who perform abortions. Abortions in the United States are normally performed by medical doctors; how many doctors would be willing to risk loss of medical license plus criminal penalties? It might be that non-doctors would rush in to fill part of the demand. But the question I'm discussing at the moment is whether laws against abortion would notably reduce the number of abortions. When physicians (all but a few of them) stop performing abortions openly and legally, and they're replaced by illegal and covert non-physicians, who can doubt that the number of abortions will decline in a very notable way? As for the objection that such laws will not *totally* do away with abortion, and are therefore ineffective — well, laws against murder, rape, and bank robbery do not *totally* do away with murder, rape, and bank robbery, but does anybody doubt that our rates of murder, rape, and bank robbery are much lower than they would be in the absence of such laws?

Someone might argue that driving physicians and legal clinics out of the abortion business will probably result in the deaths of many women, and therefore, to prevent this grave evil, Catholics should tolerate abortion. To this charge several answers could be given. First, the numbers are vastly disproportionate: saving the lives of more than a million unborn babies per year versus the loss of life of a small number of women.[82] Second, the deaths of these women would be an unintended byproduct of laws against abortion; abortion wouldn't be prevented *by means of* these deaths. By contrast, the lives of these women could be saved *by means of* allowing the homicide of millions of unborn children. Third, given the immense experience with abortion in America in the last few decades, and given the great advances in remedial medicine that have been made in the same period, it's unlikely, even in the hands of non-physicians, that illegal abortions would be nearly as risky to women as they were in the pre-*Roe* era.

In the end, then, there seems to be no good Catholic reason why Catholic voters and legislators should not attempt to pass laws that ban or at least limit abortion. Abortion is a violation not of Church-made law but of Natural Law, and none of the standard exceptions for tolerating grave violations of Natural Law seem to apply: abortion is not harmless, and laws against it will be neither ineffective nor counterproductive. Our conclusion, therefore, must be (*pace*, Mario Cuomo) that Catholics, along with conservative Protestants, Mormons, Jews, and Muslims of like mind, have a right to try to "impose" their abortion beliefs on society.

[82] Some will object that this is a very "hard-hearted" calculation. Maybe it is, but the question under discussion at the moment is *what* the Catholic position is, not whether it's hard-hearted.

Appendix V

American Jews and the Culture War

If American Jews, politically considered, aren't very significant in numbers, they're far from insignificant when it comes to political ideas and political influence. Although they might be no more than two percent of the overall population, they make up a far greater percentage of the population of American intellectuals, as well as a greater percentage of the American upper and upper-middle classes. In what I've called the "command posts" of American culture (the national press, the entertainment industry, and elite institutions of higher education), they represent, again, far more than two percent. They're likewise disproportionately represented when it comes to political activism and to support (financial and otherwise) of political candidates. In addition to all this, they've traditionally been, and remain to this day, strong supporters of the Democratic Party — stronger even than Catholics. And so, no matter how much I'd like to keep things brief, in a book about politics and religion in America, it's fitting to say something about American Jews.

It's further fitting in a book mainly devoted to American Catholics, since in the course of American history there have been strong resemblances between the two groups. Both were originally "strange" or "alien" from the point of view of the overwhelmingly Protestant majority. Both faced prejudice and discrimination; both, remembering their European histories, feared persecution; and both surrounded themselves with metaphorical "walls" to protect themselves from outsiders and to promote in-group solidarity and mutual aid. Psychologically speaking, both were able to guard against feeling inferior to the ascendant Protestants by reminding themselves that they had special status in the eyes of God, a status Protestants didn't have: the Jews claimed to be God's "chosen people" and the Catholics claimed to belong to God's "one true Church." And, of course, both groups were predominantly Democratic when it came to political party preferences.

Jews in America may be roughly divided into three groups:

- *Orthodox Jews:* those who belong to the traditional rabbinic Judaism that commenced in Palestine over two thousand years ago. There's a super-strict and super-traditional subdivision of Orthodoxy, the Hasidim (often called "ultra-Orthodox"), who emerged in Eastern Europe a few centuries ago and now mostly live in and around New York City.

- *Religiously liberal Jews:* I'm including adherents to both Reform Judaism and Conservative Judaism in this category. Like liberal Christians, they periodically amend the content of their religion so that it will keep in step with modern "progress." They desire a form of Judaism that's a *via media* between Orthodoxy and anti-religious secularism. Historically speaking, Reform Jews have been more prompt than Conservative Jews to accommodate to modernism; but both groups have been accommodationists, i.e., religious liberals.

- *Jews who are outright secularists:* they're quite nonreligious or anti-religious, either atheists or agnostics, but they continue to think of themselves as Jews — and they're thought of as Jews by other Jews. A person can't very well be an atheistic Christian (this would be a contradiction in terms), but one can be an atheistic Jew. For Judaism is an ethnicity as well as a religion; or more accurately, for Jews there's no separation between ethnicity and religion. To be a Jew is to have an inherited membership in a sacred community.

From the mid-nineteenth century on, among Jews who considered themselves religious believers, the liberals (i.e., Reform or Conservative) have far outnumbered the Orthodox. There were two reasons for this. For one, when Jews first came to America in significant numbers, they came from Germany, and in Germany Judaism had at that time already begun to transform itself into a liberal religion. It wasn't until the late nineteenth century, when great numbers of Eastern European Jews flooded into America, that Orthodoxy truly established itself.[83] In stark contrast to American Protestantism, where traditionalism came first and liberalism only much later, in American Judaism, liberalism preceded traditionalism.

At all events, religious Jews have usually been liberal rather than Orthodox; and from this it follows that Jews have been more likely than Christians to end up as secularists. Why? Because, as I've argued earlier in the book (see the chapter "Liberal Christianity"), religious liberalism has little staying power; it's a halfway house to complete infidelity. It will serve for a generation or so for

[83] Jews who had come to America in the colonial period were Orthodox, but they were very small in numbers.

those believers who have no stomach for orthodoxy but are not yet psychologically or morally prepared to take the complete leap into secularism; however, what the parents consider too great a leap, their children and grandchildren will find a relatively small step. This is as true among Jews as among Christians: once you abandon traditional or orthodox religion, you're on a slippery slope toward secularism. Among Jews of the first half of the twentieth century, this tendency toward secularism was reinforced by the socialist ideas with which many of them became infected while still living in Russia.

The result of all this is that the percentage of American Jews who are secularist is higher than the percentage of non-Jews who are secularist. This isn't to say, however, that most Jews are secularists; nor is it to say that most secularists are Jews; even less is it to say that secularism is chiefly a Jewish phenomenon. (I've noticed that those who criticize secularism are sometimes accused of using *secularist* as a euphemism for *Jew* — and then, of course, these anti-secularist critics can be denounced as anti-Semites.) I think there can be no doubt that the clear majority of American Jews, although religious liberals, aren't secularists. Nor are most secularists Jews; rather, secularists tend to come from Christian families.

Now, in the Culture War the main battle is being fought between secularists and old-fashioned Christians, but a secondary battle is being fought between secularists and old-fashioned Jews. And just as it makes little or no sense for traditional Catholics and Protestants to support a Democratic Party that has become the ally of the secularist enemies of their religion, so it makes little or no sense for Orthodox Jews to support that party either.

Not only does it make no sense for Orthodox Jews to support the Democrats; in the long run, it makes little sense for Jews of any kind to do so. The advance of secularism tends to undermine and destroy the Jewish community in America. This is because the Jewish community replenishes itself not by making converts but through intermarriage and childbirth: Jews marry other Jews and have Jewish children. But secularized Jews are more likely than their religious counterparts (whether liberal or Orthodox) to marry non-Jews, diluting both the Jewish identity and, over time, the size of the Jewish community. The result of increasing secularization is that the Jewish community, to the degree that it's non-religious, weakly religious, or religiously liberal, will shrink in size.

Indeed it's already shrinking, and if present trends continue, it might eventually fade away to almost nothing. If the Jewish community in the United States is to survive and flourish over the long run, Jews will have to practice in-group marriage to a far greater degree than they do at present; but recent American history (since the 1960s) shows they tend not to practice in-group marriage unless they're strongly religious — that is, at or near the Orthodox end of the spectrum. If secularism prevails in American culture, Jews, no less than Christians, will find it difficult to be religious, which means they will find it difficult to be Jewish.

Secularism, then, isn't just the enemy of Christians and Orthodox Jews; it's the enemy of the survival of the Jewish community in the United States — a far greater enemy than old-fashioned American anti-Semitism ever was.

Biographical Note

David R. Carlin

A lifelong Democrat, David Carlin was a Rhode Island state senator from 1981 to 1992, serving as senate majority leader in 1989 and 1990. In 1992 he was his district's Democratic candidate for the U.S. House of Representatives.

For over twenty years he has been a professor of philosophy and sociology at the Community College of Rhode Island.

Carlin's previous book, *The Decline and Fall of the Catholic Church in America*, is available from Sophia Institute Press. In addition, he has published more than a hundred articles on social, political, and religious topics, writing for the *New York Times*, *America*, *Homiletic and Pastoral Review*, *First Things*, and other journals, secular and religious.

Carlin and his wife, Maureen, live in Newport, Rhode Island.

Sophia Institute Press®

Sophia Institute is a nonprofit institution that seeks to restore man's knowledge of eternal truth, including man's knowledge of his own nature, his relation to other persons, and his relation to God. Sophia Institute Press® serves this end in numerous ways: it publishes translations of foreign works to make them accessible for the first time to English-speaking readers; it brings out-of-print books back into print; and it publishes important new books that fulfill the ideals of Sophia Institute. These books afford readers a rich source of the enduring wisdom of mankind.

Sophia Institute Press® makes these high-quality books available to the general public by using advanced technology and by soliciting donations to subsidize its general publishing costs. Your generosity can help Sophia Institute Press® to provide the public with editions of works containing the enduring wisdom of the ages. Please send your tax-deductible contribution to the address below. We welcome your questions, comments, and suggestions.

For your free catalog, call:
Toll-free: 1-800-888-9344

Sophia Institute Press®
Box 5284, Manchester, NH 03108
www.sophiainstitute.com

Sophia Institute® is a tax-exempt institution as defined by the Internal Revenue Code, Section 501(c)(3). Tax I.D. 22-2548708.